YOSEMITE NATIONAL PARK

★★★★★★★★★★★★★★★★★★★★★★★★★★★★★★★★★★★★

Edited by ROBERT SCHARFF
with the cooperation of the
NATIONAL PARK SERVICE

★★★★★★★★★★★★★★★★★★★★★★★★★★★★★★★★★★★★

DAVID McKAY COMPANY, INC.
NEW YORK

YOSEMITE NATIONAL PARK

COPYRIGHT © 1967 BY ROBERT SCHARFF

All rights reserved, including the right to reproduce this book, or parts thereof, in any form, except for the inclusion of brief quotations in a review.

foreword

BETWEEN 1867, when Alaska was purchased from Russia, and 1869, when the Golden Spike wedded the Coasts with a band of steel known as the transcontinental railroad, something of uncelebrated significance occurred, and now—as we approach its centennial—we should take note of it: A man walked into California. It was 1868.

His name was John Muir, and though it is possible, it is quite unlikely another man has lived in this country who loved the wilderness as much. He wrote of ". . . the mighty Sierra . . . so gloriously colored, and so radiant, it seemed not clothed with light, but wholly composed of it, like the wall of some celestial city." But, unlike Emerson and Thoreau, Muir went beyond mere writing: He sensed that to protect this vision, this place of retreat and renewal for the human spirit, what he called "legislative interference" would be necessary, and out of his efforts a crusading organization, the Sierra Club, came into being.

Millions of Americans have visited Yosemite. Millions of others will do so in our tomorrows, down the years. Few will know the name Muir, though the magnificent Yosemite Valley is itself a monument to his fight and foresight. But most will be seeking, each in his own way, what Muir knew and loved: Wilderness. This, a hundred years ago, was the single most influential factor in American life. This, today, is yet recognized as an elemental force whose benefits are there for those who seek them, but whose benefits must still be fought for. For, as John Muir counseled:

> "Climb the mountains and get their good tidings. Nature's peace will flow into you as sunshine flows into trees. The winds will blow their own freshness into you and the storms their energy, while cares will drop off like autumn leaves."

This is so, as all of us who have climbed mountains know full well.

And this is deserving of our continued efforts, for it is both life and beauty!

STEWART L. UDALL
Secretary of the Interior

acknowledgments

To put a book like this together requires a great deal of help. And I certainly received it from the National Park Service and the concessioners at Yosemite National Park. Superintendent John M. Davis and members of his Yosemite Park Service staff, including William A. Schnettler, Bryan Harry, Edgar P. Menning, William R. Jones, and Coyt H. Hackett, helped greatly in the gathering of material and checked both the manuscript and proofs for accuracy. In addition, I should like to thank Douglass W. Hubbard (former Chief Naturalist at Yosemite National Park) and William Perry of the National Park Service in Washington, D. C., for their invaluable assistance. I am indebted to the Yosemite National History Association, Inc., for use of certain materials from their publications.

Hilmer Oehlmann, Henry P. Berrey, John F. Curry, and Chan Russell of the Yosemite Park and Curry Co., have been especially helpful in the preparation of the book.

ROBERT SCHARFF

Contents

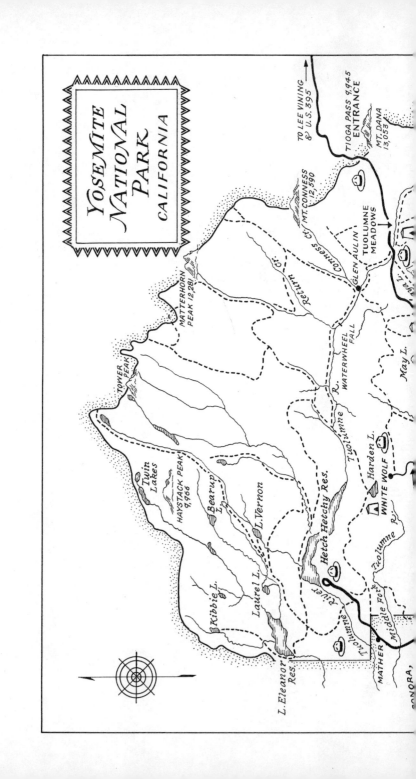

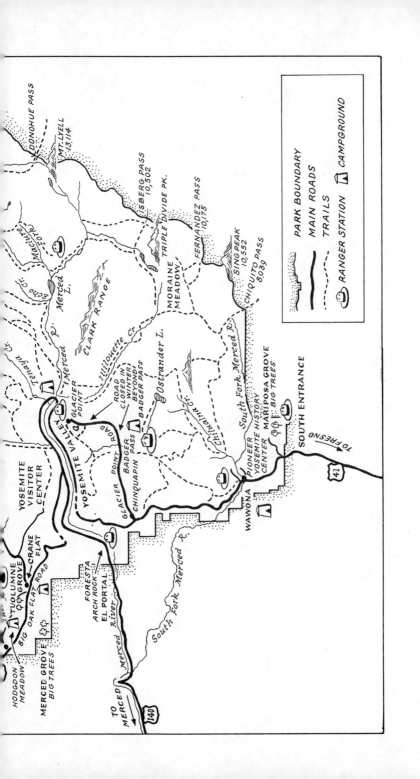

Chapter 1.

Yosemite: High, Wide, and Unbelievable

YOSEMITE! What pictures the word calls forth! Headlong water-falls, shining cliffs, dancing rivers, and soaring domes! Un-rivaled among beauty spots is Yosemite. One can stand in its center, at the foot of Yosemite Falls, and possess within a day's tramp in any direction more scenes of exquisite beauty and more natural objects of thrilling interest than anywhere else on the globe.

Yet the Yosemite Valley proper, in which occurs the greatest concentration of beauties and wonders, is comparatively small: a stage of nature but a mile broad and eight long—so small and intimate, in fact, that if the side walls folded over on the valley beneath they would almost completely cover and conceal it. But beyond those walls are other beauties, other wonders, so widely distributed that this larger, less-known area of Yosemite National Park can claim hundreds of touring and camping parties at a time without any one party having the slightest knowledge of the other.

This magnificent pleasure land lies on the west slope of the Sierra Nevada Mountains. The crest of the range is its eastern boundary as far south as Mount Lyell. The rivers which water it originate in the everlasting snows. A thousand icy streams con-verge to form them. They flow west through a marvelous sea of peaks, resting by the way in hundreds of snow-bordered lakes,

---

Yosemite Falls is without doubt the best-known attraction in the Park. The total height of its three falls is 2,425 feet. Yosemite Park and Curry Co. photo   1

romping through luxuriant valleys, rushing turbulently over rocky heights, swinging in and out of the shadows of mighty mountains.

The Yosemite Valley occupies 8 square miles out of a total of 1,189 square miles in the Yosemite National Park. The Park above the rim is less celebrated principally because it is less known. It is less known principally because it was not opened to the public by motor road until 1915. And even now, except for several leading into the valley, there are only two roads above the rim. Of these, only one crosses the Park from side to side.

For the rest, the Park includes, in naturalist John Muir's words, "the headwaters of the Tuolumne and Merced Rivers, two of the most songful streams in the world; innumerable lakes and waterfalls, and smooth silky lawns; the noblest forests, the loftiest granite domes, the deepest ice-sculptured canyons, the brightest crystalline pavements, and snowy mountains soaring into the sky twelve and thirteen thousand feet, arrayed in open ranks and spiry pinnacled groups partially separated by tremendous canyons and amphitheaters; gardens on their sunny brows, avalanches thundering down their long white slopes, cataracts roaring gray and foaming in the crooked rugged gorges, and glaciers in their shadowy recesses, working in silence, slowly completing their sculptures; new-born lakes at their feet, blue and green, free or encumbered with drifting icebergs like miniature Arctic Oceans, shining, sparkling, calm as stars."

Now nearly two million people every year, from every corner of the world, spend summer, spring, autumn, or winter vacations here, for Yosemite is a year-round park.

Nowhere in the world are there waterfalls of such variety within a single area as those that leap into Yosemite Valley in the spring and early summer. Each has its own particular beauty, but perhaps the most overpowering, when in full flow, are the Yosemite Falls, whose combined height of 2,425 feet makes them the second highest in the world. (Angel Falls—3,212 feet—in Venezuela is the world's highest.)

The domes and granite rocks of the valley—whether in the glow of sunset or the darkness of a gathering storm—invite awe and

---

From Wawona Tunnel viewpoint, the whole of Yosemite Valley is spread out in an arresting panorama. To the left is the gigantic monolith of El Capitan; at center is the great bulk of Half Dome; at right is the beautiful waterfall of Bridalveil Fall. Yosemite Park and Curry Co. photo

admiration. Add to these the groves of Giant Sequoias, the alpine meadows, lakes, and snowfields of the High Sierra, and you will understand why these wonders continue to draw people back to Yosemite again and again. And just as you never tire of looking, you probably will never find time to do all the things the Park invites, such as hiking the mountain trails, riding horseback in the valley or on the heights; fishing in the valley and in the high country; swimming and sunning on the river beaches; and skiing on the slopes at Badger Pass in winter. You can picnic, or camp and sleep beneath a starry sky, or you can luxuriate at any of a number of comfortable hotels. Though parts of the valley are sometimes crowded, it is easy to find solitude and quiet.

It will take many visits for you to know Yosemite, but whatever the mood or season, it will not disappoint you.

YOSEMITE'S HUMAN STORY

Long before the coming of the white man, Yosemite Valley is believed to have been inhabited by Indians. But with the ravages of wars and sickness the Ahwahneeches, a once-powerful tribe—and one of the last to occupy the "deep, grassy valley"—became practically annihilated. The few disheartened survivors left the area to affiliate with other neighboring tribes.

After many years in which the valley remained unoccupied, a young and adventurous Indian by the name of Tenaya, who claimed to be a direct descendant of the Chief of the Ahwahneeches, and who had been born and raised among the Monos, decided to return to what he considered his homeland. From the Monos, Paiutes, and other tribes, he persuaded remnants of the Ahwahneeches to join him, and with a band of approximately two hundred he reoccupied the valley, naming himself as chief. These Indians represented a small part of the Interior California Miwoks, a complex of tribes which in ancient times numbered in the neighborhood of 9,000, composed of closely related tribal groups occupying the western foothills and lower slopes of the Sierra Nevada.

In accordance with Indian tradition, Tenaya's tribesmen were separated into two divisions—the "Coyote" side and the "Grizzly Bear" side. Outsiders eventually designated the whole tribe as "U-zu-ma-te," which means "Grizzly Bear." (From the phonetic pronunciation of the Indian word U-zu-ma-te the region's name Yosemite is derived.) The Indian term for the valley itself remained

Ahwahnee (deep, grassy valley), as it had been so called by the earlier Ahwahneeche inhabitants.

Ahwahnee was only the summer home of Uzumates. The climate was mild enough so that all they needed were tepee-like shelters called *uma-chats*—made from bark of the incense-cedar trees—which protected them from summer rains. When winter snows fell, however, most of the Uzumates moved to the foothills.

For a few score years Tenaya reigned supreme in Ahwahnee and the surrounding area. Then in his declining years came the California gold rush. Wherever mining activities flourished, Indian supremacy quickly vanished. Driven from their home, they sought another dwelling place, only to be routed out again and again with further aggression of the whites. Their final destination was to be the Indian reservations.

Nearer and nearer came the greedy gold-seekers to Tenaya's domain. Such towns as Mariposa, Mount Bullion, and Coulterville sprang up with suddenness when gold discoveries drew throngs of white men to their vicinities. While Indians of the foothills made treaties with the whites, many mountain Indians, including the Uzumates, resented their intrusion. In retaliation and in a futile effort to discourage the white men from further usurping their lands, a number of Indian outrages were committed, some of which were charged directly to the Uzumates.

In March 1851, under the authority of Governor McDougal, the Mariposa Battalion was organized to subdue the Uzumates and their neighboring tribes, and to convey them to the Fresno River Reservation where Indians of the San Joaquin Valley and the coast had already been established by the Indian Commissioners. This fighting force was under the command of Major James D. Savage, a veteran of the Mexican War. After the Mariposa Battalion had surprised and captured an Indian rancheria on the South Fork of the Merced River at what is now called Wawona, Major Savage sent an Indian messenger ahead to demand that Tenaya surrender, emphasizing that it would be to the advantage of the Uzumates immediately to sign a treaty with the Indian Commissioners to quitclaim their lands, and to leave for the reservation on the Fresno River without resistance.

Upon Tenaya's advice, the Uzumates agreed to make treaty, and the old chief himself went on ahead to report to Major Savage that his people were coming in. Major Savage waited three days for the fulfillment of Tenaya's promise, and then, suspecting him of deceit, took part of his company and set out toward the valley

with Tenaya acting as guide. Following along an old Indian trail in the approximate location of the present Wawona Road, they came midway upon a scattered line of seventy-two Indians. There were old squaws, younger women with papooses on their backs, small children, but no braves. All were weary from the long march over and through snow several feet deep. Although Tenaya assured Major Savage that this group represented his entire tribe, the major was still suspicious. He sent Tenaya back to the South Fork Camp with the Indians, while he and his soldiers went on to search for the rest of the Uzumates.

Through Major Savage's grim determination to rout out the Indians from their mountain refuge, members of his fighting force, on March 21, 1851, became the first white men to enter the Uzumate's Valley, though William Penn Abrams and U. N. Reamer had probably seen it from the south rim in 1849, and members of the Joseph Reddeford Walker party may have looked in from the north rim in 1833.

The Mariposa Battalion failed that day in its expressed purpose (a second expedition under Captain John Boling did capture the remaining Indians), but its members upon their return home aroused public interest and curiosity in the wonders and beauties of the area.

In 1855, James Mason Hutchings, an English adventurer, and two Indians guided the first tourist party into Yosemite country. On his return, Hutchings wrote the first published account of the wonders of the valley for the *Mariposa Gazette*. He had been accompanied by Thomas Ayres, Yosemite's first artist, whose sketches appeared with Hutchings' writings in the *California Magazine* in July 1856. They attracted hardy visitors to Yosemite from all over the United States.

By 1864 private enterprise threatened the valley's beauty and free access, so certain farsighted Californians had Senator John Conness (for whom one of the High Sierra peaks beyond Tuolumne Meadows is named) introduce a bill into the United States Congress that would require the State of California to preserve and protect Yosemite Valley and the Mariposa Grove of Giant

---

One of the most memorable experiences of Yosemite is to watch the clouds wreathe about the cliffs at the time of clearing storms. Here the high cliff of Half Dome rises above the snow-covered winter forests of Yosemite Valley. National Park Service photo

7

Sequoias in a natural, undisturbed condition. Passed by Congress, it was signed by President Abraham Lincoln on June 30, 1864, and provided that there be granted to the State of California:

The "Clift" or "Gorge" in the Granite Peak of the Sierra Nevada Mountains known as the Yo-Semite Valley . . . as well as the Mariposa Grove of Big Trees . . . for public use, resort and recreation . . . inalienable for all time.

When the State accepted, this was the first practical application of the idea that has resulted in today's great National Park System.

A Board of Commissioners was appointed by the governor, and the new State Park's first guardian was Galen Clark, who in 1856 established Clark's Station, in an area known today as Wawona. He served from 1866 to 1879. James Mason Hutchings, who meanwhile had become the father of the first white child (Florence) to be born in the valley, was the Park's next guardian (1880-1884).

Though only rough Indian trails led to Yosemite in early times many visitors came to see and breathe in the spectacular scenery. But, as the years went by, toll roads penetrated into Yosemite Valley, permitting a slightly more comfortable mode of entry than horseback riding. Two roads were completed in 1874, a third the following year, and the stages began to descend the steep talus slopes in the valley's west end. In 1877 the Yosemite Stage and Turnpike Company was established as the first organized stageline in Yosemite. The first automobile reached Yosemite Valley in 1900, and the first entrance permit (good for 7 days) was sold for $5.00 in 1913, the same year a motorized stageline began operation. Earlier, in 1907, the Yosemite Valley Railroad had been completed to El Portal at the Park's western boundary, where visitors transferred to stagecoaches for the trip up the steep canyon. Later, the stages were replaced by buses. Floods, the decline of the local lumber industry, the closing of one cement mine and the barium mines, and the growth of mass auto travel with the completion in 1926 of the All-year Highway (the Merced Road or Route 140) up the Merced Canyon led in 1945 to the demise of this interesting mountain railroad.

In the years following the Yosemite Grant of 1864 many hostelries were operated to take care of Yosemite visitors. The Cosmopolitan in the Old Village was considered by some to be the finest saloon and bathhouse in the state. Other old hotels included

An early-day stage descending into the Valley. The trip was a slow, rough, and dusty one at best. The stages first entered the Valley on this road in 1875. National Park Service photo

Leidig's, Upper, Black's, Hutchings', La Casa Nevada, and the Stoneman House. Competition in those days was a dog-eat-dog affair but, once the summer season was over, getting a cup of coffee often was an impossibility. Through survival of the fittest, descendants of several of the early concessioners serve you in Yosemite National Park today. Degnan's Restaurant dates back to 1884 when John Degnan worked for the Yosemite Valley Commissioners and his wife's home-baked bread was eagerly purchased by hungry travelers. David Curry, the "Stentor of Yosemite," opened Camp Curry in 1899. Artist and photographer Harry Best's studio began as a tent in the Old Village in 1902. The largest of all Yosemite concessioners and the one providing all overnight accommodations, excepting the free campgrounds, is the Yosemite Park and Curry Co., a stock corporation formed by merger in 1925 of the Curry Camping Company and the Yosemite National Park Company.

In 1868, a gentle, Scottish-born naturalist, John Muir, came to the valley as a young man. Appalled at the destruction caused by grazing, he began to write about the need of conservation in wilderness areas, and in the late 1880's found a sympathetic publisher in Robert Underwood Johnson of *Century Magazine*. Between them, they influenced Congress and the American people to think in terms of National Parks. Thus in 1890, again by an Act of Congress, Yosemite National Park was established *around* the original Yosemite Grant. This (National) Park around a (State) Park was administered by the United States Army. The State of California continued its control of the original grant until 1906, when it re-ceded its lands to the Federal Government, and the dual administration ended.

Members of the cavalry were a common sight in the National Parks' early days. It was logical to call upon this branch of the United States Army to patrol the Parks. In Yosemite, this was summer duty only, and the march to and from the Park from their winter base near San Francisco normally required fourteen days each way. Cavalry headquarters was at Camp A. E. Wood at Wawona and later at Fort Yosemite, near the present Yosemite Lodge.

By 1914, civilian supervision was in effect. When the National Park Service was founded on August 25, 1916, by Act of Congress which was signed by President Woodrow Wilson, its first director was Stephen T. Mather, a Californian and a great friend of Yosemite.

ADMINISTRATION OF THE PARK

Yosemite National Park is administered by the National Park Service, United States Department of the Interior. Affairs within the Park are directed by a superintendent, assisted by personnel trained in the fields of protection, interpretation, maintenance, and administration, and their duties include most of the operations ordinarily performed by state, county, and local governments.

The superintendent in the Park is personally responsible for the establishment of broad policies and for the success of overall management, including maintenance of satisfactory public-service standards by private concessioners operating within the Park. This is done within National Park Service guidelines, and with the assistance of National Park Service staff specialists when necessary. The superintendent is aided by an assistant superintendent. While there are four major divisions in the Park operations—administration, maintenance, ranger services, and interpretation—the latter two are the ones a visitor usually meets. The superintendent of Yosemite National Park, whose address is Yosemite National Park, California 95389, is also in immediate charge of Devils Postpile National Monument (see page 176).

Park headquarters, in Yosemite Village, is open 24 hours a day. Report fires, accidents, lost persons, injuries, or any other emergencies there.

PARK RANGERS

Uniformed Park Rangers are responsible for enforcement of rules and regulations in the Park, fire detection and suppression, operation of entrance stations, and general supervision of activities in the several districts into which the Park is divided. They also handle lost and found property and receive suggestions and complaints from visitors.

If you are in any sort of difficulty or need information, see a Park Ranger. He is there to help you. You will find them at entrance stations, ranger stations, and patrolling roads and campgrounds. Remember, however, that he is also a Park police officer, commanding the same respect you give such an officer at home. He is authorized to issue summons for the violator of a Park regulation to appear before the U. S. Commissioner at Park headquarters. Persons who commit more serious offenses may be tried in the U. S. District Court.

PARK INTERPRETIVE SERVICE

In Yosemite, as in the other scenic areas of the National Park System, there is a varied interpretive program which will surely help you to greater knowledge and understanding of both the natural and the human history of the Parks. The program includes exhibits at the visitor centers, guided walks, campfire programs, informal talks, and accurate, easy-to-read literature. Specific details on the interpretive program are found in Chapters 3, 4, and 8. Remember that Park Naturalists, who are also in uniform, are the Parks' interpretive force. They are here to help you understand what you see in the Parks, and they are responsible for all interpretive services, which are free of charge.

It was at Yosemite that the "Nature Guide" idea was introduced into the National Park Service. Out of it has come a distinctive interpretive program which last year served some ten million people in the National Parks and historical areas and a still bigger total in State Parks. It is hardly necessary to explain that this work has its good effects upon public appreciation of parks and the protection of our national heritage.

The man responsible for bringing the Nature Guide idea to America is Dr. Charles M. Goethe, who, with his wife, prior to World War I observed nature guiding being done at Switzerland's "Lake of the Four Forest Cantons." In the early part of 1919 the Goethes used their personal funds in organizing a nature-guide program at Lake Tahoe.

Regarding this Dr. Goethe wrote, "Six resorts ringed the lake. At one, Fallen Leaf, the owner was a longtime friend, W. W. Price, who had majored in biology at Stanford. He immediately saw the possibility of what Mrs. Goethe and I were attempting. He converted reluctant owners of the other five resorts to the idea of extending hospitality to the two naturalists who conducted the Tahoe nature walks. So these naturalists covered the six resorts, one a day, each week."

The naturalists referred to were Harold Bryant, then with the California Fish and Game Commission, and Loye Holmes Miller, University of California, Los Angeles. This was in the summer of 1919, and by great good fortune the work was observed by Director Mather. Dr. Goethe reports, "Going to register, at Fallen Leaf, he passed the crowded auditorium and missed supper. It happened that that evening's lecturing naturalist was Dr. Miller. He had rare ability to call wild birds. His talks on their music

12

packed Fallen Leaf auditorium that night. Folks stood outside the windows. Seeing this popular outpouring induced Stephen Mather to ask transfer of our experiment to Yosemite National Park." Regarding the transfer Dr. Miller writes, "Mr. Mather asked me to confer with him on the subject of nature-guide work in Yosemite and urged me to come at once to the Valley. It was late in the season and I had spent most of my free time for the year . . . I therefore urged Mr. Mather to wait until 1920 for the inauguration of an official Nature Guide Service. He agreed and we parted with a definite plan for 1920."

The definite plan for 1920 saw Harold Bryant first on the job. Dr. Miller arrived soon afterward. Between them they offered the first public interpretive work of the National Park Service. In 1921, Miller and Bryant again combined their efforts. Enid Michael joined them as ranger-naturalist. Ansel F. Hall, a year-round Ranger in Yosemite, had been busy assembling the collections for a Yosemite Museum which was opened to visitors at this time. By 1922 a Park Naturalist Department was formally created with Hall in charge—a forerunner of the interpretive program which quickly spread to all major scenic parks with a counterpart in historical areas.

HOW TO REACH THE PARK

About the size of the State of Rhode Island, Yosemite National Park is located in central California on the western slope of the Sierra Nevada. This mountain range was named by the Spanish settlers after the Sierra Nevada (or snowy range) in southern Spain, the highest mountain range in that country.

By Automobile. From the north and west, take U. S. Route 99 to Merced; then California State Route 140 (open all year) into Yosemite Valley via Arch Rock Entrance Station. Another interesting route, though slower, is over the Big Oak Flat Road (State Route 120) from Manteca. This road, which enters via Big Oak Flat Entrance Station, is also open all year.

From the south, State Route 41 from Fresno enters the Park near Wawona at South Entrance Station, and sweeps down to the Valley. This entrance, which is open the year around, takes you near the Mariposa Grove of Giant Sequoias. The distance from Merced to the Valley is 81 miles and from Fresno, 94 miles.

From the east, the Tioga Pass Road (State Route 120) from Lee Vining (on U. S. Route 395) via Tioga Pass Entrance Station, open from late May till the first snows, is an easy drive through a panorama of granite peaks.

By Railroad and Bus. The Southern Pacific and the Santa Fe railroads and the Western Greyhound and Continental buses operate to Merced and Fresno from the north and south. The Union Pacific (rail) and Western Greyhound buses connect from Reno via Harvey's Wagon Wheel to Lake Tahoe.

The Yosemite Transportation System of the Yosemite Park and Curry Co. carries many passengers to Yosemite Valley from Fresno and Lake Tahoe in summer and from Merced all year. (Write to Yosemite Transportation System, Yosemite National Park, California 95389, for timetables, or visit your local travel agent.)

By Air. United Air Lines between Los Angeles and San Francisco makes scheduled stops at Fresno, Merced, and Reno. Pacific Air Lines between Los Angeles and San Francisco makes scheduled stops at Fresno. Consult air service timetables for connections with Yosemite Transportation System.

ENTRANCE FEES

Yosemite National Park has been designated as a recreation fee area pursuant to the Land and Water Conservation Fund Act of 1965.

1. *Annual Recreation/Conservation Permit*—This $7.00 permit admits the individual paying such fee and all those who accompany him in a private noncommercial automobile. This permit is good until March 31 of the year following issuance and admits the purchaser to all National Parks, National Forests, and other federal areas designated as "recreation fee areas."

2. *Daily and 30-Day Permits*—Shorter-period permits are available, but exact fees vary. For information inquire at Park entrance stations. All of the above permits are authorized by the Land and Water Conservation Fund Act of 1965.

Should the entrance station be closed for any reason, the fee may be paid at Park Headquarters in Yosemite Valley where there is a ranger on duty 24 hours a day. The entrance fee collected is without any guarantee that space is available in the campgrounds or accommodations, or that any other service or facility is available. No refunds can be made nor can the fees paid under one of the options be applied subsequently as partial payment of the fees under another option. The permit must be in possession when entering and leaving the Park. Replacement of any permit that has been lost, misplaced, stolen, or destroyed will require payment of desired permit. No refund can be made for unused fees.

YOSEMITE'S SEASONS

Yosemite National Park is open every day in the year and each season has its own distinctive beauty.

Summer. In the summer—family vacation time—the rock walls of Yosemite Valley seem to groan trying to harbor the crowds. Campgrounds are crowded from mid-June to early September, and other facilities are often in use beyond their intended capacity. July and August are good months to go into the high country. There the meadows are colorful with the season's first flowers, for spring is late up there. The magnificent water wheels of the Tuolumne River are whirling 30 to 40 feet into the air, and you can almost hear things growing.

In the valley, days are usually warm; nights are pleasantly cool. Shady trails make hiking and riding comfortable pastimes. In mid-summer, river beaches are fine for sunning. It seldom rains between June 1 and September 30, except for occasional afternoon thundershowers.

Autumn. Indian summer is a lovely season in Yosemite. In September the ferns in the valley begin to turn a hundred shades of gold and yellow; in October the trees turn tawny, and the air crackles with the first frost. Fishing is at its best, for streams and lakes are low, and the fish are near the surface.

Autumn color of oak and maple, dogwood and aspen varies from year to year, and with different elevations. By the end of October the Big Oak Flat and Wawona Roads are often in riotous display. Color along the 58-mile stretch of the Tioga Road from Crane Flat to the pass comes earlier and is an unforgettable sight. Check with the Chief Ranger's Office (phone 372-4466) to find out whether or not the road is blocked by snow.

Winter. Center of winter outdoor activities at Yosemite is the Badger Pass ski area, reached by way of the south entrance from Fresno and the west entrance from Merced. It is 20 miles from Yosemite Valley on the Glacier Point Road. Ski season is from about mid-December to mid-April, depending on weather. Have tire chains available.

You will find slopes for skiers of every degree of skill. The most popular is that from the upper terminals of the chair lift and

Number 1 T-bar. Others, such as those served by Numbers 2 and 4 T-bars are preferred by the novice skier. Ski school is in session daily. Marked ski trails through the woods nearby are maintained by the National Park Service. (See Chapter 7 for more details on winter activities in the Park.)

Spring. The season of waterfalls! Spring in Yosemite Valley means May and June, when the waterfalls are booming all around, the leaf buds are bursting in a pattern of green, and the dogwood and azalea reveal themselves in showy white and pink along the roadside. Sometimes melting snow and spring rains bring dozens of temporary waterfalls into play and swell the waters of the major falls to many times their average volume. During these periods of heavy flow, Yosemite is a photographer's paradise.

Normally, temperatures in Yosemite Valley are quite mild. During the summer daytime temperatures sometimes reach 100°. Nights are *cool.* Winter temperatures range from the high 40's, with an occasional mid-60° reading, to the mid-20's . . . with readings sometimes as low as 5° to 10° above zero. (Record low was −6° in 1924.) Precipitation varies greatly with a record in 1938 of 59.01 inches of moisture to 14.77 inches in 1924. Normal for Yosemite Valley is 36.51 inches. The first snow of the season usually comes to the Valley sometime after November 15, and the last snow sometime before April 15. Yosemite Valley receives an average 74 inches of snow during a winter season. Normally, the snow does not get over two feet deep, although it has on rare occasions attained a depth of five feet.

Average Precipitation and Maximum and Minimum Temperatures—
Yosemite Valley

MONTH	PRECIPITATION	MAXIMUM	MINIMUM
January	6.35	47	25
February	6.64	55	26
March	5.07	58	30
April	3.29	65	34
May	1.48	71	39
June	0.51	80	46
July	0.29	89	50
August	0.06	89	50
September	0.55	82	48
October	1.68	72	39
November	3.49	57	30
December	7.10	49	26

Chapter 2.

Geology of Yosemite

THE FIRST view of Yosemite Valley is a sight to inspire reverence. From the deep shadows of the pines, a silent compelling vista bursts upon the eye. Mighty rock sentinels guard the entrance and beyond them towering cliffs and verdant valley swim in a glorious light.

On the south wall shimmers the Bridalveil Fall. The water slips over the great granite wall, white and ethereal. It seems to drop its tenuous mist into the very tree tops. Often the wind swings the great column of Bridalveil Fall from the face of the cliff and waves it like a scarf or veil. On the north wall, Yosemite Falls leaps out of a smooth channel and falls some 2,425 feet to the Valley below.

Around the shoulder, behind which Bridalveil Creek makes its way to the brink, tower the Cathedral Rocks. They get their name from a resemblance in outline to that of the Duomo at Florence, and rise 2,680 feet above the valley floor. Just beyond them are seen the Cathedral Spires, one solitary shaft of granite uplifting for more than 700 feet.

Across the narrow valley, and nearly opposite, is El Capitan—a rock more than twice as great as Gibraltar. It rises 3,564 feet, with an apparently vertical front. Thrust out like a buttress, it presents to the vision an area of more than 400 acres of naked granite. Sublime and steadfast it stands, a veritable "Rock of Ages." The bulk of El Capitan is so stupendous that it can be seen from a vantage ground 60 miles distant.

Eagle Peak, in the Three Brothers group, lies a little beyond El Capitan. Its height is 3,773 feet. Sentinel Rock faces the Three Brothers from the south wall, a splintered granite spire, very slender, and nearly perpendicular for about 1,500 feet below its apex,

17

its total height being 3,068 feet. Back of this natural and majestic monument stands Sentinel Dome, its storm-worn top 4,157 feet above the valley.

Across the valley from Yosemite Falls the massive shoulder of Glacier Point is thrust out from the south wall, and, almost opposite, on the north, stands Yosemite Point, flanked on the east by Indian Canyon, once used by the Indians as exit or entrance for Yosemite.

The Royal Arches are near the head of the valley, in the vast vertical wall whose summit is North Dome. The arches are recessed curves in the granite front, very impressive because of their size, and made by ice-action. Much of the rock has developed in layers like the structure of an onion, the arches being the broken edges of these layers. Washington Column is the angle of the cliff at this point—a tower completing the massive wall at the very head of Yosemite.

Over against it, but looking down the valley, stands the highest rock of all the region—Half Dome, as it is called. It is 8,842 feet above sea level, or 4,748 feet above the valley floor. Its massive front is fractured vertically for about 2,000 feet, and the face turned outward is polished by wind and storm—a mountain apparently cut away by some mighty giant's scimitar. The side of the Half Dome toward the southwest has the curve of a great helmet, so smooth and precipitous as almost to defy the climber. On its overhanging rock, however, the most venturesome have stood. From hotels and camps, Half Dome is often seen raising its head above the clouds.

To the northeast from here opens Tenaya Canyon. Mirror Lake, an expansion of Tenaya Creek and lying between the North and Half Dome, is at the entrance. When the sun creeps over the great flank of the Half Dome, the whole landscape is wonderfully reproduced in this miraculous mirror, the reflection of the sunrise being an unusual feature. But sunrise over these colossal cliffs is much later than the sunrise at lower levels.

Bridalveil Fall, one of the most beautiful and better-known of Yosemite's waterfalls, drains Bridalveil Creek and is never completely dry. Indians called this fall "Pohono" or puffing winds. When summer breezes waft the water of Bridalveil across the face of the cliff you can see why it was given its name. The Cathedral Rocks, or Three Graces, form the majestic backdrop for the Fall. Yosemite Park and Curry Co. photo

After visitors have recovered from their first shock of astonishment at the beauty of the Valley, they inevitably wonder how nature made it. How did it happen that walls so enormous rose so nearly perpendicular from so level a floor?

HOW THE VALLEY WAS FORMED

More than 200 million years ago the area now occupied by the Sierra Nevada was covered by a shallow arm of the Pacific Ocean. While thus submerged great quantities of sand and silt, brought down by the streams of the neighboring continent, were deposited on this ocean floor in successive beds to a depth of several thousand feet. Then there came a change which caused the ocean floor to be lifted and be transformed into dry land. At the same time the beds of sand and silt, hardened to rock, were compressed into gigantic folds, or wrinkles, thousands of feet high, and thus was created a mountain system composed of many parallel ridges with north-westerly trend. Under the arches of this mountain system welled up in viscous molten form the granite which you see here on every hand. During the long periods of time that followed (more than 100 million years) these ancient earth wrinkles were slowly worn down by streams, rain wash, and other agents, until at last the bulk of the original sedimentary material was thus stripped away and the granites exposed over large areas. Remnants of the older sediments, now considerably altered and folded, still exist today, particularly along the crest of the Sierra and in the lower foothills. A geological marker has been placed at one of these sites on the all-year highway from Merced to Yosemite about 10 miles west of Arch Rock Entrance Station. There may be seen the broken and intensely folded strata that represent the oldest rocks of the Yosemite region.

For a long time thereafter the Sierra region was a lowland, and then it began slowly to bulge up, together with the country to the east. Finally, more violent convulsions in the interior of the earth caused the crust to break into huge blocks. Some of these blocks were pushed or tilted and began to stand out as mountain ranges, others settled back and gave rise to intermediate valleys. Thus came into existence the ranges and intermediate valleys of what is termed the Great Basin, which includes most of Utah, Nevada, and eastern California.

The largest and westernmost of these many tilted blocks is the Sierra Nevada range. It is actually a single block some 400 miles

El Capitan is the largest exposed monolith of granite in the world, twice the height of Gibraltar. Yosemite Park and Curry Co. photo

long and 80 miles wide with a north-south trend. The Sierra block's uplift has been effected by a rotation on its long axis. On the east it presents a steep scarp, while on the west it slopes gently to the Great Valley of California. But this tilting did not take place in one gigantic upheaval. There were many gradual upward movements, separated by great lapses of time, and finally two distinct periods of more rapid upthrusting. Since then there have been only occasional minor disturbances, and the range as a whole has been essentially stable. The last noticeable movement occurred in 1872, at the time of the Inyo earthquake. The range then lifted 20 feet, or, to put it another way, Owen's valley on the east dropped 20 feet. At any rate, a fresh break 20 feet high is visible for miles along the eastern foot of the Sierra Nevada.

With the beginning of the uplift the streams that had found their ways about the surface of the region naturally rearranged themselves on the Sierra block. The long westward slant resulted in master streams flowing down the slope to the Pacific. With successive uplifts, the slope became steeper, and the steeper the slope became, the more rapidly the rivers flowed. The greater the velocity of the streams, the deeper were the canyons they cut. The Merced and the Tuolumne Rivers, two of the master streams that are now within Yosemite National Park, were affected exactly as were the others. The powerful rush of their waters from the heights carried boulders, gravel, and sand which added scouring forces and rapidly deepened their beds. It has been determined that the Merced in the region of Yosemite Valley had in this manner cut its canyon to a depth of more than 2,000 feet. Like all water-cut canyons, the Merced gorge was V-shaped in cross sections.

Then came a change in climate. Winter conditions prevailed on the mountain tops for many thousands of years. It was at this time that the great Ice Age came on. On the Sierra, snow accumulated to the depth of more than 1,000 feet. The weight of this mass caused it to compact to form granular ice. Such ice, present in great fields, is plastic like tar. Under the action of gravity, long tongues or rivers of it flowed down from the continuous fields on

---

Royal Arches, North Dome and Washington Column. The Royal Arches are beautiful glacier-cut arcs of granite, on the face of the north canyon walls. The thickness of the overhang varies from 10 to 80 feet. The vertical wall of Washington Column rises 1,952, and North Dome towers 3,571 feet, above the floor of the Valley. National Park Service photo

23

the heights, and ground with irresistible force into the V-shaped canyons that the streams had cut. These ice tongues pushed down to altitudes of 2,000 or 3,000 feet above sea level, where their advance was halted by melting. The stream-cut canyon in the region of the present Yosemite Valley was entered by two glaciers, each more than 2,000 feet thick, one through the main gorge of the Merced, and the other through Tenaya Canyon. The mighty trunk glacier, formed by their union, filled the chasm to its brim and pushed down to the vicinity of El Portal. In the region above the "rim," evidences of this early ice invasion are found in disintegrating moraines—rock debris.

There is clear evidence of two invasions and less distinct evidence of a third and still earlier one. The protracted occupation of Yosemite Valley by the above-mentioned glacier was followed by a long period of milder climate, during which the ice melted away. This interval between glaciers probably lasted for hundreds of centuries. Then there came a recurrence of glacial climate, and again the ice occupied the Yosemite Valley. This latest glacier reached no farther than Bridalveil Meadow and filled the Valley only one-third of its depth. It was relatively shortlived and accomplished much less in excavating than did the earlier ice.

For hundreds of centuries this glacier held sway, quarrying and scouring the sides and floor of the chasm through which it flowed. The old V-shaped canyon was wiped out of existence. In its place was formed a fairly vertical walled trough, rounded at the bottom, and in places more than 3,000 feet deeper than the stream-cut canyon. Fully twenty thousand years have elapsed since the ice withdrew from Yosemite Valley. However, in one sense, the glacial epoch has not yet ended, for on the Sierra crest a few small glaciers still hold their own.

As a result of glaciers, the narrow stream-cut canyon has been transformed into a broad U-shaped trough; the craggy slopes were quarried back to vertical cliffs; tributary streams (except Tenaya Creek) were left in hanging valleys from which they poured their waters over brinks of cliffs; and a basin was scooped out in the rock floor of the Valley, in which was formed the ancient Lake Yosemite. The depth of glacial excavation ranges from 600 feet at the lower end of the valley to 3,000 feet at the head.

Cathedral Spires (left). These graceful, yet frail looking granite rock forms stand 1,950 and 2,154 feet above the Valley floor. The Three Brothers are at the right. National Park Service photo

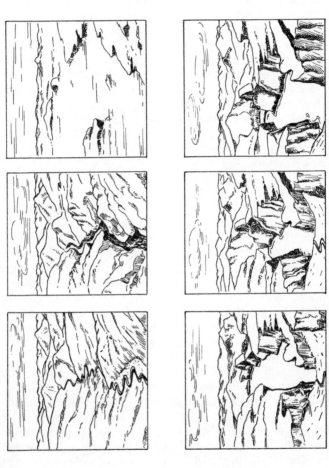

*The formation of Yosemite Valley at a glance. (Left to right; top to bottom):
The broad valley era; the canyon era; the first glacial stage; the last glacial
stage; the ancient Lake Yosemite; and Yosemite Valley today. Courtesy of
Yosemite Natural History Association.*

In its descent from the heights the glacier carved a giant stairway—vertical steps alternating with horizontal treads. Over two of these treads the river now plunges to produce Vernal and Nevada Falls. Many other steps, less spectacular but of the same origin, exist at higher levels. On many of the horizontal treads are water-filled basins. Merced and Washburn Lakes are examples. At the very summits of the range, where the glaciers had their birth, another characteristic of glacier action is to be noted. Where the ice came in contact with the cliffs of the valley heads, a plucking action was carried on by the ice. Great bowl-shaped hollows or amphitheaters, called cirques, were quarried out by the glaciers. Hundreds of examples are to be seen on Yosemite peaks. Part of the rock material plucked from the cirques and canyons was dropped along the margins of the glaciers in the form of lateral moraines that, in places, ridge the "rim" of the gorge.

Because the Merced River flowed directly down the long slopes of the Sierra, it has from the beginning intrenched itself more rapidly than have its tributaries. Yosemite Creek, for example, flows parallel to the long axis of the range. Successive uplifts of the Sierra block caused the master stream to flow more rapidly, so cutting its canyon deeper. These uplifts did not affect the velocity of Yosemite Creek. Consequently, its valley lagged behind, and when the Merced had intrenched itself in a V-shaped trough 2,000 feet deep, Yosemite Creek still flowed along the surface above. At the edge of the sloping, walled canyon the creek tumbled in a cascade to the river below. With the coming of the glaciers the same principle held true. The small ice mass that occupied the Yosemite Creek basin could not keep up with the excavating process of the mighty glacier that ground through the master stream canyon. When the ice melted, Yosemite Creek was left hanging higher than ever on the walls of the gorge. Furthermore, because of vertical joint planes in the granite, the former sloping sides of the canyon were transformed by the ice to tremendous vertical cliffs over which Yosemite Creek plunged to form one of the world's most wonderful falls. Falls formed by other streams tributary to the Merced in the region of Yosemite Valley have a similar history.

At first thought it appears an anomaly that the comparatively feeble Tenaya Creek should have intrenched itself 2,000 feet deeper than did the master stream in the region of Little Yosemite Valley. (Little Yosemite Valley is the valley of the Merced River between Nevada Fall and Merced Lake.) At the head of Yosemite

Valley, Tenaya Creek debouches at nearly the same level held by the Merced River. Here is one tributary that was not left suspended in a hanging valley.

The natural joints in the Yosemite granite have had much to do with the varied configuration brought about by the ice and water. In places the joint planes are vertical, in other places they are horizontal, occasionally they are neither horizontal nor vertical but at an angle between, and in still other localities the rock is solid. In the case of Tenaya Canyon, the joint planes were numerous in various directions, and both stream-cutting and glacial-quarrying were facilitated. In spite of its lesser power, the Tenaya glacier kept up with the main glacier in its cutting. On the other hand, the rock under the Little Yosemite Valley is but very sparsely fractured and consists of great horizontal sheets. These the mighty Merced ice tongue could not quarry away block by block but could only rasp and polish.

As has been explained, the great variety in configuration of Yosemite walls is due to the distribution and spacing of the joints. Where cracks were numerous, the rock yielded readily to the modeling action of ice and water; where no cracks existed, the rock stubbornly resisted change. In the case of El Capitan, there is presented a wonderful example of a solid rock mass. Any cracks that existed were sealed with molten material that welled up from below. Likewise, the remaining structure of the Cathedral Rocks is, for the most part, unbroken by joints. Their very solidity made them invulnerable even to such inconceivable power as that exerted by the grinding flood of ice. The gorges above and below the Yosemite Valley are narrow because carved from very solid rocks.

About 20,000 years ago when the Yosemite ice melted, it left a splendid example of a basin cut in granite. On the rock sill enclosing this basin the terminal moraine of the last ice invasion had been formed. The moraine served as a natural dam and behind it water from the melting ice masses above the valley backed up to make a lake 5½ miles long. No human eye ever looked upon that lake, for as soon as it had formed, natural processes began to destroy it. The streams which flowed into it were heavily laden with sediment brought from the scouring ice masses above. A great delta grew out into the upper end of the lake, and from a geological standpoint it was but a short time before it was filled in. It is upon that sand, gravel, and boulder fill that we walk today. It has been computed that this fill is over 2,000 feet deep in Yosemite

28

Beautiful Hetch Hetchy Reservoir in Yosemite, since 1913 in exclusive use of the City and County of San Francisco as their water supply. National Park Service photo

Valley. Could it all be scooped out, it would be found that the original bottom of the rock trough cut by the ice is U-shaped.

The lake that existed in Little Yosemite Valley was filled in the same manner. Merced Lake, Washburn Lake, and others of the high-country lakes are experiencing the same destruction.

Surprisingly few other changes have taken place in post-glacial times. The great walls about Yosemite Valley have lost their polish through the years of weathering. A number of great rock slides have taken place, but, as a rule, only small talus slopes have formed along the cliff bases. In view of the great verticality of the cliffs, it is surprising that more wholesale breaking down has not occurred. The Merced River is constantly changing its meandering course, which process brings about noticeable changes on the Valley floor, but these evidences of change are short-lived. Forests and other vegetation claim a place, and the change they bring about is quite marked. In all probability, man-made "improvements" are the most notable changes in the program at present, and most of these would fade into nothing should man disappear and the Yosemite be returned to its primitive state.

HETCH HETCHY VALLEY

The Tuolumne River follows a tumultuous course westward across the Park a few miles north of the Tioga Road. It has a larger drainage system and more water volume than the Merced. Its Waterwheel Falls is one of the most interesting wonder's of scenic America. Its Grand Canyon will stand high among America's beautiful canyons. Its valley, the Hetch Hetchy, has been, while not so famous as Yosemite, a "celebrity" for some years.

Hetch Hetchy Valley is generally recognized as being analogous to Yosemite though on a smaller scale. The profound gorge of the Tuolumne, with its stepped profile of bare, glaciated rock emerges suddenly on a wide, flat-floored, sandy valley, just as Tenaya Canyon opens on Yosemite. Both valleys have had the same history. Glacial abrasion and plucking over-deepened the canyon, so that, when the ice retreated, a tarn occupied the basin. This tarn served as a trap for sediments brought down from the melting ice above,

Sentinel Rock on the southern rim of the Valley rises some 3,086 above the Valley floor. Just west of the Rock, Sentinel Fall can be seen in the spring and early summer. National Park Service photo

and the filling of the basin built out the level floor of Hetch Hetchy. The reservoir created in Hetch Hetchy Valley by O'Shaughnessy Dam at its outlet is but a restoration on a larger scale of the lake which once was there. Incidentally, the term "Hetch Hetchy" is derived from a Miwok or Paiute Indian word that denotes a kind of wild food that once abounded in the valley in the days when the Indians made it their home.

DOMES AND PINNACLES

Yosemite's granite domes are unsurpassed anywhere in the United States, perhaps in the world, for number and variety. How were they formed? In two ways:

First is by exfoliation (from the Latin "to strip of its leaves"). When overlying layers of rock were worn away, the release of pressure caused internal strain which in turn developed a system of cracks in the granite (like the layers in an onion). Weathering caused these shells or layers to peel off. Thus, gradually the angular surfaces took on a rounded contour, eventually producing the "domes." Their scaly surfaces, on both a large and small scale, tell us that exfoliation is still going on.

The best examples of such domes are Sentinel Dome (you can climb it easily from a spur off the Glacier Point Road), Turtleback Dome (on Wawona Road), and the Starr King group, which can be seen clearly from Sentinel Dome or from along the Glacier Point Road. All these were fashioned long before the glaciers came.

In the formation of certain other domes, however, overriding glacial action also played a part in the rounding process. Near Tenaya Lake and Tuolumne Meadows, as you drive toward Tioga Pass, you can see clusters of domes, varying in size and symmetry. Look for the "glacier polish," on which the backlight of early morning or late afternoon gleams as it would on sheets of ice. Watch, too, for the "erratics," which are rocks and boulders of all sizes, brought down from the mountaintops by glaciers and deposited on the smooth glaciated surfaces when the ice melted away.

"Where is the other half of Half Dome?" is a question sometimes asked by Park visitors. There never was another half Dome; that is, no other half of solid granite. At one time more material existed where the blank, north face of the dome now stands, but this material was cracked into vertical sheets. The ice in crowding

32

Vernal and Nevada Falls. National Park Service photo

through Tenaya Canyon quarried into these giant slabs and carried them away. Incidentally, George C. Anderson, a blacksmith, was the first man to climb Half Dome in about 1875. He made iron eyebolts which he drove into cracks on the back side of Half Dome. Sometimes he had to hook his big toe over one spike while he reached up to drill and drive the next one. Today you can climb to the top of Half Dome safely by means of a double cable (see page 85).

There are many evidences of glacial action on or near the Valley floor. At the El Capitan and extending across the Valley to Cathedral Rocks is a splendid example of a terminal moraine. The auto road which crosses the El Capitan Bridge is cut into the eastern slope of the ridge. This moraine was formed by the ice of the last invasion and played an important part in the post-glacial history of Yosemite Valley. Below El Capitan Bridge, on the south side of the river, is a part of this moraine which has been cross-sectioned by the highway builders. In this cross-section one may view the components of the moraine which range from finest glacial flour to boulders the size of a house. At the turn of the road leading to Bridalveil Fall is a very prominent remnant of a terminal moraine.

In Little Yosemite Valley a series of small terminal moraines, dropped by the Merced Glacier in its dying days, may be seen less than a half-mile above Nevada Fall. A great series of lateral moraines exists on the slopes above Little Yosemite Valley, and examples may be viewed from the Merced Lake Trail a mile or so above Merced Lake Camp. Moraines in the making will be found below the Lyell Glacier.

Small patches of polish and striae may be seen on the granite walls of Yosemite Valley above the gravel pit at Rocky Point, near the spring behind the old chapel, and in Tenaya Canyon just above Mirror Lake. At higher altitudes, as at Tenaya Lake and Merced Lake, great, shining areas of polish will be seen. The Indians called Tenaya Lake "Py-we-ack," Lake of the Shining Rocks. Early geologists found polish that had been left by the earlier ice invasions on the Wawona Road near Artist Point. Unfortunately, the ledge upon which this rare relic existed was blasted out by road workers. Specimens of the polish are preserved at the Yosemite Valley Visitor Center.

The rock pavements and domes along the Merced River above Yosemite Valley and along the Tioga Road are well decorated with precariously perched boulders left by the melting ice.

34

The basin that existed on the floor of Yosemite Valley immediately after the glacier melted was a typical but very large tarn. Above Vernal Fall in the course of the river is a small pool (Emerald Pool) which may be considered a tarn. In Little Yosemite Valley a lake once existed which experienced a history similar to that of the ancient Yosemite Valley Lake. Merced Lake, Washburn Lake, and hundreds of High Sierra lakes are good examples of glacial tarns.

From Glacier Point one obtains a magnificent panorama of peaks and slopes. A number of amphitheatres, quarried by ice, are visible from there. Any trip on High Sierra trails will bring one to vantage points where numbers of cirques may be viewed. On those peaks where glaciers are still active, one may witness the process of cirque-making.

YOSEMITE'S WATERFALLS

In spectacular waterfalls, Yosemite Valley is supreme. Nowhere else on the North American continent are there high mountain streams with such varied and beautiful courses. Because of the very high cliffs they fling their waters over the crests in spectacular falls and unite in a valley river. In May and June the falls are at their fullest when the winter snows are melting. They are still full in the beginning of July, but after that decrease rapidly in volume. But let it not be supposed that the beauty of the falls depends upon the amount of water that pours over their banks. It is true that the May rush of water over the Yosemite Fall is even a little appalling. The ground sometimes trembles with it half a mile away. But the spectacle of the Yosemite Fall in late August is equally fascinating. In August, specially in dry seasons, much of the water reaches the bottom of the upper fall in the form of mist. The sight is quite unique. So Yosemite offers the visitor two seasonal "faces" —one of great bulk and power, the other uplifting in its delicate beauty.

Thanks to an excellent system of roads in the Valley—including the one to Glacier Point—you may receive excellent views of all but two of the principal waterfalls. And even these—Illilouette Fall and Snow Creek Falls—can be seen from points along the Valley's trails.

Regardless of what road brings you into the Valley, a waterfall is bound to strike your eye. Entering from the south by means of

Wawona Road (Route 14) you will behold Bridalveil Fall. This is a mountain torrent dropping 620 feet into the Valley's embrace. In falling, the stream of water "floats" gracefully. The slightest breeze can bear the Fall twenty feet or more from its direct downward course in one direction or the other. As evening approaches, Bridalveil tosses the gayest of rainbows about its shoulders. This fall can be viewed to good advantage from several locations, particularly from the parking area near its base, from the esplanade at the east portal of the Wawona Tunnel, and from Valley View on the Valley Loop Road.

When entering the Park from the west on the Merced Road (Route 140), you will observe Wildcat and Cascade Falls (500 feet) about three miles after passing the Arch Rock Entrance Station. They descend gracefully over the irregular granite walls on the north side of the Valley; and while in reality only cascades, they are impressive and beautiful. Both can be viewed safely from a parking area provided along the road.

Near the junction between the Big Oak Flat and Valley Loop Road—just before reaching the base of El Capitan—you may witness during the spring and early summer the Park's highest single fall—Ribbon Fall (1,612 feet). Unfortunately, this high fall is one of the first to dry up as July approaches. Speaking of spring, El Capitan is often enhanced during this portion of the year by numerous small rivulets of water from the melting snows upon its crown that stream over the edge of this giant precipice, dissolving into a fine spray in mid-air.

The most famous waterfall in the Park is, of course, Yosemite Falls. As previously stated, the total height is 2,425 feet. It is divided into three parts—the upper fall of 1,430 feet, or a height equal to nine Niagara Falls piled one on top of the other; a middle cascade of 675 feet; and a lower, 320 feet, or two Niagaras more. Yosemite Falls can be seen to advantage from many locations, each presenting a different dramatic effect. Most noteworthy of all is the one you receive from along the short trail that parallels Yosemite Creek, just above Yosemite Lodge. Other good views may be obtained from various spots on the South Valley road, from the front of the Yosemite Visitor Center, and from Glacier Point.

Two other water drops that can be viewed from Glacier Point are Vernal (317 feet) and Nevada Falls (594 feet). Vernal is extremely picturesque; the black rocks about its sides are covered with ferns, and there is an eternal spray which makes it possible for rainbows to dance about the pool at its base. A very interesting walk from Happy Isles (see page 46) is along the "mist trail" at its side. Above Vernal Fall the Merced River comes coursing down a long glissade of granite from the base of thunderous Nevada Fall, whose waters seem to leap straight out of the sky. Nevada Fall is the first mighty leap of the Merced River on its way from the high Sierra snowfields to the sea. Both waterfalls were named in 1851 by Dr. Lafayette Bunnel, surgeon with the Mariposa Battalion.

Yosemite Valley is the abiding place of other waterfalls scarcely named or noted, yet so lofty and beautiful that they would each be famous in some other setting. Royal Arch Cascades (1,250 feet) can best be observed from the meadows between Camp Curry and the Ahwahnee Hotel; Staircase Falls (1,300 feet) may be seen above and in back of Camp Curry; Silver Strand Falls (1,170 feet) may best be viewed from the esplanade at the east portal of the Wawona Tunnel; and Lehamite Falls, a comparatively less dramatic series of cascades in Indian Canyon which are most advantageously observed from in front of the Park Visitor Center.

Another series of cascades is Sentinel Falls (2,000 feet), which descends to the Valley floor through a deeply cut recess on the South Valley wall just west of Sentinel Rock. Actually, this drop consists of two principal portions—the upper which is composed of a group of minor falls dropping from a series of rock ledges, each being from 50 to 200 feet in height, and the lower section made up of a more or less clear drop of over 500 feet.

Other regions of Yosemite National Park also have their own beautiful and interesting waterfalls, but they suffer by comparison with those of Yosemite Valley. In the Hetch Hetchy section, for instance, we find Wapama (1,500 feet) and Tueeulala (1,000 feet) Falls. The Tuolumne Valley also abounds in many interesting cascades, including previously mentioned Waterwheel Falls. While not "falls" in the same sense as the others in the Park, Waterwheel is worth a visit. A hike of eight miles from Tuolumne Meadows takes you to a point about three miles below Glen Aulin on the Tuolumne River (see page 103). At this point in the river, rock obstructions in the river bed hurl the waters 30 to 40 feet into the air in a series of giant "wheels" that extend down the steeply inclined canyon for over a mile. The best time to see Waterwheel Falls is during times of high water, usually in July. Lesser of these river "wheels" are located on the Silver Apron above Vernal Fall and on the Merced River several miles below Merced Lake.

MINERALOGY OF THE YOSEMITE REGION

By far the greater part of the area of the Yosemite National Park is made up of a single type of rocks, the granites and others closely similar to them. They make up the massive walls of Yosemite and the several ranges in the central part of the Park.

Granite is the most common of the so-called plutonic rocks. These rocks were formed by the cooling of a molten mass. They differ from the lava rocks that form at the surface by the fact that the hot fluid (magma) from which they formed cooled within the earth rather than at the surface. The depth at which this took place was certainly several miles—some geologists say about 11 miles. Under these conditions the cooling is a very slow process, and as a result the granites are rather coarse-grained rocks.

With the unaided eye it is possible to distinguish several of the minerals that go to make up the granite. (It may be well to state here that minerals are definite chemical compounds occurring in nature usually in crystallized form, and rocks are assemblages of one or more [usually more] of these minerals. These definitions are somewhat inexact, but no satisfactory definition of either rock or mineral has ever been given.) Even a hasty glance shows that the granite is made up mostly of light-colored grains with a few dark ones scattered through it. There are three light-colored minerals that go to make up most of the rock. Quartz, a glassy, colorless or white mineral that occurs in rounded grains and breaks with a rough surface, is most easily recognized. Plagioclase is also white or colorless but shows a smooth break or cleavage and is often striated. It usually has a prismatic outline and is not so glassy as quartz. Orthoclase is similar to plagioclase but is not infrequently pink or greenish and does not show any striations. Sometimes it is made up of a very fine lattice of more or less transparent parts. Plagioclase and orthoclase both belong to the feldspar group, and it is often difficult to tell them apart.

Two dark minerals are usually prominent in the granite, mica and hornblende. When perfectly fresh and in thick pieces they are

---

These famous Waterwheel Falls are three miles below Glen Aulin High Sierra Camp on the Tuolumne River and about an eight mile hike from Tuolumne Meadows. The falls are named from huge "waterwheels" caused by the river bottom ledges which throw the water high into the air. National Park Service photo

both quite black, but in thin slivers they are dark green or brownish green. The mica occurs in lustrous flakes that can be split very thin and are then quite flexible. The hornblende is usually in short columns with flat faces and is quite hard and brittle. A very close inspection of the granite sometimes reveals two other minerals. One is magnetite, magnetic iron oxide, that will jump to the magnet if removed from the rock. It occurs in minute rounded black grains. Another is titanite, a mineral that is particularly characteristic of the granites of the Sierra Nevada. It is usually a dark honey-yellow and forms minute crystals with smooth faces and rounded edges.

No important mining has been carried on within the limits of the Park, but just outside both to the east and the west rich mineral deposits have been found. On the west the gold belt of the foothills stretches northwestward from the vicinity of Mariposa for over a hundred miles. A part of this is sometimes called the mother lode. It is a belt characterized by thick veins of massive white quartz in and adjoining which occurs the gold ore. Much of the gold is native, and some of the largest nuggets ever found have come from this region. On the east, there has been some gold mining in the Tioga Pass area. But, only a few of the most favorably situated mines in Yosemite country are still operating at a profit, though the hope for a further large production is by no means dead among the inhabitants of the old mining towns.

Ribbon Fall is formed by the waters of Ribbon Creek as they plunge into a recess of the canyon wall a little west of El Capitan.
National Park Service photo

Chapter 3.

Seeing the Park by Auto

THE FIRST car to enter Yosemite Valley was a Stanley Steamer driven by Frank H. Holmes and his brother, Arthur E. Holmes, of San Jose, California. It was in July of 1900 that they made their arduous trip by way of Madera and Raymond. But, the general use of automobiles in *all* National Parks was forbidden until 1913. The Coulterville Road was opened to automobiles in 1913, while their use on the Big Oak Flat and Wawona Roads was not permitted until a year later. Today there are nine major roads which will take you to most of the important features of Yosemite National Park.

On the major roads of the Park, roadside posts locate, identify, and explain the important features. These posts—primarily installed to be used with the Yosemite Natural History Association's booklet, *Auto Tour of Yosemite National Park* (see page 202)— are given a *letter* (V for Yosemite Valley Loop Road, G for Glacier Point Road, etc.), which is followed by a *number* for each point of interest. These are noted on the cumulative mileage tables for the various roads. For instance, V27 identifies El Capitan, G8 indicates Sentinel Dome, etc. Incidentally, while cumulative mileages are used in the tables in this chapter, remember that speedometer mileages will tend to vary between individual automobiles.

The first car to enter Yosemite Valley was this Stanley Steamer driven by Frank H. Holmes of San Jose, accompanied by his brother, Arthur E. Holmes. It was in July of 1900 that they made their arduous trip by way of Madera and Raymond. The auto body was built especially for the Yosemite trip. National Park Service photo

As with the roads in all National Parks, those of Yosemite are designed to provide beautiful vistas and to take the visitor to points of great interest. While the *maximum* speed limit is 45 miles per hour in the Park, plan at least one hour for each 25 to 30 miles of roadway to be covered. Travel leisurely and stop often to view the points of interest. But, when stopping, be sure to park only in the space provided off the roadway. Roadside posts, or points of interest, indicated in the cumulative mileage tables given in this chapter that are marked with an *asterisk do not have safe parking spaces provided.

Except for Tioga Road and Glacier Point Road beyond Badger Pass, all Park roadways are kept open the year around. Tire chains or snow tires, however, may be mandatory at various times during the winter months, though the roads are usually clear except during and just after a storm. At all seasons of the year, Park Rangers patrol the roads to help motorists in difficulty.

YOSEMITE VALLEY LOOP ROAD

The 15-mile loop trip of Yosemite Valley—"The Incomparable Valley"—begins at the Yosemite Valley Visitor Center (roadside post V1) in Yosemite Village. After a stop at the visitor center, which explains the natural features and the human story of Yosemite Valley and the Park, you can follow the roadside posts either in numerical or reverse order. Of course, it is also possible to begin the tour at any location in the Valley.

After leaving the village proper, your first stop on the North Road portion of the Valley Loop will be at Glacier Point view (roadside post V2). Here, Ahwahnee Meadow offers a wide prospective to the east and south—the Royal Arches and Washington Column, Half Dome, Grizzly Peak, the Merced Canyon, and directly across the meadow, the sheer cliff of Glacier Point towering 3,242 feet above the valley. This is an excellent spot from which to view the famous Glacier Point firefall (page 175). On the other side of the road from the meadows is an outdoor amphitheater, "Church Bowl," where religious gatherings are held in summer.

Continuing on, the road goes south past Ahwahnee Gate (entrance to the Ahwahnee Hotel) and then turns east. Traveling along this stretch of road, you have marvelous views of Half Dome, Glacier Point, Sentinel Rock, and the Cathedral Rocks. You will cross the Merced River twice within a short distance. Near the second bridge, the large tree growing on the bank is the largest sugar pine in Yosemite Valley. A little further on, a short spur road branches to the left and Indian Caves.

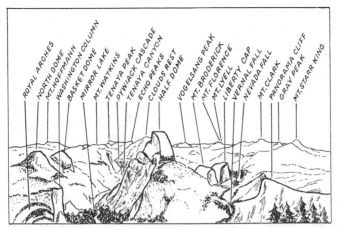

ROYAL ARCHES
NORTH DOME
MT. HOFFMANN
WASHINGTON COLUMN
BASKET DOME
MIRROR LAKE
MT. WATKINS
TENAYA PEAK
PYWIACK CASCADE
TENAYA CANYON
ECHO PEAKS
CLOUDS REST
HALF DOME
VOGELSANG PEAK
MT. BRODERICK
MT. FLORENCE
MT. LYELL
LIBERTY CAP
VERNAL FALL
NEVADA FALL
MT. CLARK
PANORAMA CLIFF
GRAY PEAK
MT. STARR KING

Points of interest of the Yosemite High Sierra as seen from Glacier Point. Courtesy of Yosemite Natural History Association

While the main loop road swings south a short distance past the Indian Caves, you may wish to go east along the road that follows the north bank of Tenaya Creek, by Iron Spring and then on to Mirror Lake. Named for its clear reflection of adjacent mountains (especially Mount Watkins which is reflected from the parking area side), Mirror Lake is at its best in early morning before breezes ripple the surface. The great vertical cliff above you and to the right as you face the lake from the parking-area side is Half Dome, and the promontory which juts out from behind Half Dome is the summit of the granite-sided mountain known as Clouds Rest. This mountain, so named because clouds frequently "rest" there during spring and fall, is the highest mountain visible from Yosemite Valley (9,926 feet above sea level).

Returning to the intersection of the Valley Loop Road, you turn south, crossing Tenaya Creek Bridge where there is a Government gauging station. Just past the bridge, you will come to a junction with Stable Road, which skirts a moraine known as "Ski Hill"—for it was here that skiing began in Yosemite. Continuing south, you will cross the moraine and then a bridge over the Merced River which is near Happy Isles.

At Happy Isles, the tumbling Merced River branches into several channels as it enters Yosemite Valley, forming two main islands. The name Happy Isles was originally given to this spot by W. E. Dennison, an early Guardian of the Yosemite Grant, because "no one can visit them without for the while forgetting the grinding strife of his world and being happy." Also be sure to

45

visit the Happy Isles Nature Center, an exhibit designed to enhance your understanding and appreciation of Yosemite's back country. The trails to Nevada and Vernal Falls, Half Dome, and the "back country" (see Chapter 4) begin at Happy Isles. In addition, the famous John Muir Trail (see page 108) leaves Yosemite Valley at this point, heading for Tuolumne Meadows and finally Mount Whitney, more than 200 miles away.

As you continue westward on the main Valley loop route (often called the South Road) you will pass by Stoneman Meadow, which offers a splendid view of the Royal Arches on the north valley wall. Geologists believe that arches of this type may be a step in the formation of granite domes such as North Dome on the skyline above. Washington Column is beside the arches. In the springtime and after heavy rains, Royal Arch Cascades, a 1,250-foot waterfall, streak down the cliff to the left of the Royal Arches. These arches are glacier-cut arches of granite on the canyon wall and the thickness of the overhang varies from 10 to 80 feet. The vertical wall of the Washington Column rises 1,952 feet, and the North Dome towers 3,571 feet, above the floor of the Valley. Stoneman Meadow also offers a good view of Glacier Point (directly above), and Eagle Peak and Yosemite Falls (west).

Near Stoneman Meadow and directly beneath Glacier Point, you find Camp Curry, an accommodation spot founded by Mr. and Mrs. David Curry in 1899. Near the parking area of Camp Curry there is an old apple orchard which was planted in the 1860's by James Lamon, the Valley's first true homesteader. Once passing the Camp Curry Road in a westward direction, you go by the Le Conte Memorial Lodge which is a picturesque stone building that was first built at Camp Curry in 1903 by the Sierra Club and then was later moved to its present site. The Memorial commemorates the work of Joseph Le Conte, geologist and explorer of the Sierra Nevada. Here during the summer the Sierra Club maintains a mountaineering and conservation library and exhibits, and furnishes hiking and High Sierra information.

West of the Sentinel Bridge Road junction is the site of the Old Yosemite Village. At one time, this stretch of the loop road was a bustling "main street." Because the location was subject to floods, however, the facilities of the town were gradually moved from here to present-day Yosemite Village. A few of the original buildings have been taken to the Pioneer Yosemite History Center at Wawona (see page 172) and restored; the others were razed. The only remaining building is the little Yosemite Chapel. This structure was built in 1879, and is still in use (see page 197).

The next viewpoint you will come to is that of Yosemite Falls. To the right of Upper Yosemite Fall you find the Lost Arrow which rises several hundred feet as a slender shaft of granite separated from the main cliff. Like Yosemite Falls, it owes its existence to the fracture pattern on the cliff. A series of cracks parallels the face of the Upper Yosemite Fall cliff, while another series is perpendicular. The Lost Arrow represents a shaft of granite within these two systems. The deep ravine to the right of the Lost Arrow, as seen from this viewpoint, is named Indian Canyon because it was a route of travel used by the Uzumates.

Continuing down-valley, you pass, to the left, Sentinel Rock, called "Laya" by the Indians. It rises a sheer 3,068 feet above the floor of Yosemite Valley. Just west of the Rock is Sentinel Fall. Also the Four-Mile Trail to Glacier Point cuts across its base and may be seen zigzagging up the mountainside to the east. This trail was originally constructed in 1871-72 and as its name implies it was about four miles long. Many of the first tourist accommodations were built near the foot of the trail, beginning in 1865. All that remains today of this early resort area are the locust trees planted at the site of an old well.

The viewpoints of El Capitan, Three Brothers, Cathedral Rocks, and Cathedral Spires are fairly close together. As previously stated, El Capitan is one of the greatest masses of exposed granite in the world and is 7,564 feet above sea level at its top. The face of El Capitan has been scaled by *skilled* mountain climbers but it is not recommended as a casual weekend hike. The Three Brothers are the three prominent peaks rising one above the other on the same side of the Valley as El Capitan. They were named in honor of the three sons of Chief Tenaya of the Uzumate. The uppermost is Eagle Peak, the highest point on the north rim of the Valley, standing 3,773 feet above its floor. The other two symmetrical rocks rise 2,300 and 3,000 feet. Cathedral Rocks, a large rock almost opposite El Capitan on the south rim, contains three summits which rise 1,650, 2,590 and 2,680 feet above the Valley floor. (The lowest one of these rocks, which are also sometimes called "The Three Graces," is known as "The Acorn.") Cathedral Spires are two closely set symmetrical columns in the large recess just east of Cathedral Rocks. The left spire towers 1,950 feet and the other is 210 feet higher. The spires were first climbed by expert rock climbers of the Sierra Club in 1933, but the ascent is one of extreme difficulty.

As you continue on to Bridalveil Fall, the road cuts through a glacial moraine or dam. This dam held back ancient Lake Yo-

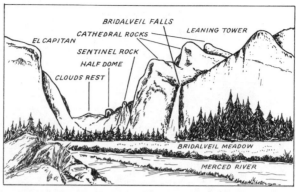

Major points of interest from Valley View near Bridalveil Meadows.
Courtesy of Yosemite Natural History Association

semite which later silted in to form the level floor of Yosemite
Valley. There is a parking area near Bridalveil Fall and if you
would like a closer look, a short walk will take you there. The
Indians called this fall "Pohono," or the "fall of the puffing
winds," and at night there is usually a warm breeze hereabouts.
Its present name, Bridalveil, was given in 1856 by Warren Baer,
editor of the Mariposa *Democrat*. While viewing the Fall, you
should note the Leaning Tower, a large overhanging rock mass
above and to the right of Bridalveil Fall. Still farther to the right
are the Cliffs of Dewey, Crocker, Stanford, and Old Inspiration
Points. On the opposite side of the Valley to the left of El Capitan
is Ribbon Fall, 1,612 feet high. Flowing mainly in spring, it is the
highest free-leaping waterfall in Yosemite.

Now to complete your loop around Yosemite Valley, you bear
right past the Wawona Road junction and go through the meadow
where the Mariposa Battalion camped (see page 7). In 1903,
President Theodore Roosevelt camped here with John Muir and
discussed conservation measures needed by our nation to help the
government protect its parks and forests.

After crossing Pohono Bridge, you turn right and a few hundred
yards will bring you to another of Yosemite's most famous vistas.
The Gates of the Valley, or Valley View as it is called today. In
stagecoach days this was the first stop for most visitors since the
roads came down the north valley wall.

After passing El Capitan Meadow and moraine—a low ridge
extending through the forest toward the river, you go by Rocky
Point, Yosemite Lodge, and Yosemite Falls, and then you will be
back at the Yosemite Valley Visitor Center—your starting point.

48

Miles	Points of Interest	Miles
0.0	Yosemite Valley Visitor Center (VI). Located in this area are the park headquarters, post office, Western Union, restaurants, grocery stores, studios, service station, garage, and other services (see page 197)	15.1
0.3	Lewis Memorial Hospital	14.8
0.4	Glacier Point View (V2). Church Bowl	14.7
0.5	Ahwahnee Gate (V3). Road to Ahwahnee Hotel (0.2 miles)	14.6
0.7	*Junction.* Middle Road (0.6 mile to Yosemite Valley Visitor Center west) and Camp Curry Road (Campgrounds #7 and #15—0.2 mile south; Camp Curry 0.5 mile south). Half Dome viewpoint (V4)	14.4
1.1	Ahwanee Bridge	14.0
1.2	Sugar Pine Bridge (V5)	13.9
1.4	*Junction.* Road to Campground #9—Yosemite Valley Youth Group Camp. (This camp is limited to organized *youth* groups only—see page 194.)	13.7
1.6	*Junction.* Road to Campground #9	13.5
1.9	*Junction* (V6). Spur road to Indian Caves	13.2
2.0	*Junction.* Mirror Lake Road (Iron Spring—0.2 mile east; Mirror Lake—0.6 mile east [V7])	13.1
2.1	Tenaya Creek crossing	13.0
2.4	*Junction.* Stable Road (Campground #12, Stables, and Kennels—0.2 mile west; Clark's Bridge—0.3 mile west; Campground #14—0.4 mile west). Glacier moraine—Ski Hill (V8)*	12.7
2.8	Happy Isles Bridge (Merced River crossing)	12.3
2.9	*Junction* (V9). Road to Happy Isles parking area	12.2
3.3	*Junction* (V10). Road to Campground #11	11.8
3.5	*Junction.* Stable Road (Campground #14—0.1 mile east; Clark's Bridge—0.2 mile east; Campground #12, Stables and Kennels—0.3 mile east)	11.6
3.6	Stoneman Meadows viewpoint (V12)	11.5
3.7	*Junction* (V11). Camp Curry Road (Camp Curry —0.1 mile south; Stoneman Bridge—0.1 mile north; Campgrounds #7 and #15—0.2 mile north)	11.4
3.9	Le Conte Memorial (Sierra Club headquarters— V13) Entrance to Housekeeping Camp (Campgrounds #16)	11.2
4.3	Merced River view (V14)	10.8

(Continued)

Miles	Points of Interest	Miles

(*Continued from page 49*)

4.7	*Junction.* Sentinel Bridge Road to Yosemite Valley Visitor Center—0.4 mile northeast	10.4
4.8	Old Village site (V15). Yosemite Chapel	10.3
4.9	Yosemite Falls viewpoint (V16)	10.2
5.5	*Junction.* Road to Four-mile Trail. Sentinel Rock viewpoint (V17)	9.6
5.6	Road to Yellow Pine, Rocky Point, and Sentinel picnic areas	9.5
6.7	*Junction.* Road to Cathedral Picnic area	8.4
6.8	*Junction.* Road to North Road via El Capitan Bridge—0.2 mile	8.3
6.9	El Capitan viewpoint (V18)	8.2
7.1	Three Brothers viewpoint (V19)	8.0
7.4	Cathedral Spires viewpoint (V20)	7.7
8.4	Bridalveil moraine (V21)	6.7
8.5	Bridalveil Fall viewpoint (V22)	6.6
8.6	*Junction.* Wawona Road to South Entrance (see page 64)	6.5 6.5
9.1	*Junction.* Spur road to Bunnell Plaque (0.2 mile) Bridalveil Meadow (V23)	6.0
9.8	*Junction.* Merced Road (Route 140) to Arch Rock Entrance Station (see page 51). Pohono Bridge	5.3
9.9	Valley viewpoint (V24)	5.2
10.7	Bridalveil Fall viewpoint (V25)	4.4
10.8	*Junction.* Road to South Road via El Capitan Bridge—0.2 mile	4.3
11.0	El Capitan moraine (V26)	4.1
11.3	*Junction.* Road to El Capitan Picnic area	3.8
11.5	El Capitan viewpoint (V27)	3.6
13.6	Rocky Point viewpoint (V28)	1.5
14.0	*Junction.* Road to Campground #4. Trailhead to top of Yosemite Falls (V29)	1.1
14.3	*Junction* (V30). Road to Yosemite Lodge. Cafeteria, restaurant, gift shop, and post office are also available	0.8
14.5	Yosemite Falls parking area (V31)	0.6
14.8	Meadow Succession interpretive sign (V32)	0.3
15.1	Yosemite Valley Visitor Center (V1)	0.0

MERCED ROAD (*Route 140*)

Descending from the 4,000-foot elevation of Yosemite Valley, the Merced Road follows the course of the Merced River past Big Oak Flat Road junction, Pulpit Rock, to Cascade Falls viewpoint. Beyond the bridge over Cascade Creek, the Merced Road has an intersection with the famous old Coulterville Road. It was the first wagon road into Yosemite Valley, and reached the valley floor only one month before the Old Big Oak Flat Road, in 1874. Both were toll roads at first. Although most of the Old Big Oak Flat Road is now abandoned, the Coulterville Road receives limited use even today. It is *very* steep and narrow, however, and exits the Park near the town of Coulterville.

Continuing westward, you pass, on the north, Wildcat Fall, where the old stage coaches were stopped to water the horses. Near here is an excellent view of Elephant Rock. After going through Arch Rock, by the Arch Rock Entrance Station and the Park boundary, you reach El Portal, where the elevation is 2,000 feet. At El Portal, there is the Pioneer Yosemite Transportation Center which tells the story of transportation to Yosemite in the post-horse era, using old vehicles and train cars from this region. Eating, lodging, automotive, and grocery services are also available here. Below El Portal the road continues along the river at a more leisurely rate of descent for 17 miles more before starting a winding climb out of the canyon to Mariposa. (Mariposa, a Spanish word meaning butterfly, was so named in 1806—perhaps during one of the migrations of butterflies that passed through the area.) From Mariposa the road descends the foothills to Merced.

Miles	*Points of Interest*	*Miles*
0.0	*Junction.* Yosemite Valley Loop Road (also called North Road) at Pohono Bridge	7.9
0.9	*Junction.* Big Oak Flat Road (Route 120)	7.0
2.6	Cascade and Wildcat Falls viewpoint (M1). Cascades Picnic Area	5.3
2.7	Cascade Creek crossing	5.2
3.2	*Junction* (M2). Coulterville Road. This old toll stage road is usable, but it is *very* steep and narrow	4.7
5.6	Arch Rock—large blocks of granite leaning together arch over the road	2.3
5.7	Arch Rock Entrance Station	2.2
7.9	Park Boundary	0.0

BIG OAK FLAT ROAD (Route 120 West)

An old oak tree, with a diameter of over 11 feet, was responsible for the naming of Big Oak Flat, an early-day mining community located approximately 30 miles west of present-day Yosemite National Park. This small town in turn loaned its name to the Big Oak Road, the second to enter Yosemite Valley. At first a toll road, it reached here in 1874, about a month after the Coulterville Road was completed. The old Big Oak Road was in use until 1945 when two giant rockslides closed its famous switchbacks to all but hikers. While the new and more direct route has eliminated the necessity of driving any of the treacherous portions of the old "paved stagecoach route," its old line of descent into the Valley is still visible, especially at Tunnel View on the Wawona Road.

While the new Big Oak Flat Road may not be as exciting as the old one, it gives many interesting views of the San Joaquin Valley, the Coast Range, and the Sierra Nevada. Starting from the junction with the Merced Road (Route 140), this road proceeds up the north wall of Merced Canyon and is routed through three tunnels along the way. After passing through the two shorter ones, it crosses Cascade and Tamarack Creeks, which join a short distance downstream to descend into the Merced Canyon as Cascade Falls or The Cascades. You also pass near Wildcat Creek which drops as Wildcat Falls into the Merced Canyon, but will only find this creek active in the spring.

Once through the longest of the three tunnels, the road circles Big Meadow to the north and joins with the old Big Oak Flat Road and the Tioga Road at Crane Flat. Crane Flat's name is nearly as obscure as its geologic origin. Early accounts indicate that sandhill and blue cranes stopped here during migration, but these were probably what we now call great blue herons. Other reports, however, say that the name comes from the Crane or Crean family, who once lived in this vicinity. Facilities at Crane Flat for summer visitors include a service station, ranger station, and public campground with a program of naturalist activities. Except for the ranger station, most of these facilities are closed during other seasons.

After this junction, the Big Oak Flat Road becomes State Route 120 and continues on down through the Merced Grove of Giant Sequoias and leaves the Park after passing Hodgdon Meadow. One mile beyond the Big Oak Flat Entrance Station, Route 120 intersects with the road to Mather and Hetch Hetchy.

Miles	Points of Interest	Miles
0.0	*Junction.* Merced Road (Route 140)	17.2
0.9	First Tunnel	16.3
1.3	Second Tunnel	15.9
1.6	Coulterville Road view (B1)*	15.6
1.7	Coulterville Road view turnout	15.5
1.9	Cascade Creek crossing (B2)	15.3
2.1	Tamarack Creek crossing	15.1
2.3	Third Tunnel. Also Bridalveil viewpoint (B3)	14.9
3.1	Merced Canyon interpretive sign (B4) and excellent view of Half Dome	14.1
3.4	*Junction* (B5). Road to Foresta Campground (2 miles). This is an organized group camp area only	13.8
7.3	Big Meadow viewpoint (B6)	9.9
9.5	Crane Flat view (B7)*	7.7
9.9	*Junction.* Tioga Road (east) and Old Big Oak Flat Road (west)	7.3
10.3	*Junction.* Road to Crane Flat Campground	6.9
10.8	*Junction* (B8). Road to Crane Flat Fire Lookout (1.5 miles on primitive road). Excellent view of San Joaquin Valley	6.4
13.0	*Junction* (B9). Road to Merced Grove of Giant Sequoias (1.5 miles on primitive road). This is the smallest of the three groves of giant trees in Yosemite National Park. It has approximately 20 sequoias	4.2
16.9	Big Oak Flat Entrance Station (B10). Also *Junction* with old Big Oak Flat Road and Hodgdon Meadow Campground	0.3
17.2	Park Boundary	0.0

OLD BIG OAK FLAT ROAD

At Crane Flat you have an opportunity to drive along one of original portions of the Big Oak Flat Road. But, because the road is fairly steep and narrow for modern traffic, it has been converted to a *downhill-only* route. This interesting drive takes you past the Tuolumne Grove of Big Trees and along the way, you receive many intimate forest views.

Miles	Points of Interest	Miles
0.0	*Junction*. Tioga Road (Route 120 East) and Big Oak Flat Road (Route 120 West)	6.5
1.0	*Junction* (O1). Spur road leads into the Tuolumne Grove of Big Trees (0.1 mile). There are approximately 25 Giant Sequoias in this grove	5.5
1.3	Giant Sequoia—directly beyond post O2	5.2
2.3	Ponderosa pine—directly beyond post O3	4.2
2.5	Incense cedar—directly beyond post O4	4.0
5.1	Sugar pine—directly beyond post O5	1.4
5.4	Hodgdon Meadow viewpoint	1.1
6.1	Entrance to Hodgdon Meadow Campground	0.4
6.5	*Junction*. Big Oak Flat Road (Route 120)	0.0

HETCH HETCHY or MATHER ROAD

The road passes through Stanislaus National Forest before entering Yosemite National Park near the Mather Ranger Station. There are two roads (one goes to the Carl Inn Campground just inside the Park and the other to Aspen Valley) enter the Yosemite from Hetch Hetchy Road. Once inside the Park, the road goes through Poopenaut Pass (name of unknown origin) and into the valley of the same odd title. (This valley is noted for its abundance of Pacific rattlesnakes.) Farther along you come to Hetch Hetchy Reservoir.

Here, behind O'Shaughnessy Dam, the Tuolumne River floods Hetch Hetchy Valley, which many claimed was comparable in beauty to that of Yosemite Valley before its inundation. The proposed damming of the Tuolumne caused one of the greatest battles in conservation history. While some individuals insisted that the water was necessary for the future growth of San Francisco and the Bay Area, conservationists led by John Muir said that it was "incredible" to dam up "one of Nature's rarest and most precious mountain temples." But, the conservationists, as so often is the case, lost their fight and the dam was built during the years 1914 to 1923. In 1938, the dam was raised to its present height. At high water, the crest is 312 feet above the original riverbed, while the reservoir extends up the valley more than 8 miles. The water is employed to produce hydropower and is then sent 172 miles by an aqueduct to San Francisco for its use by the city.

On the north side of the valley, you will note two waterfalls dropping into the reservoir. The closer one is Tueeulala, while

54

Wapama is a little farther on. (In the summer, Tueeulala often dries up.) While at Hetch Hetchy, take the short walk to the center of the dam and see the plaques that give the statistical details of its construction. This spot also provides a view of the prominent formation known as Kolana Rock on the south side of the Valley.

Miles	Points of Interest	Miles
0.0	*Junction.* Route 120	17.0
1.1	*Junction.* Road to Carl Inn Campground. Also South Fork of the Tuolumne River Crossing	15.9
2.1	*Junction.* Road to Aspen Valley—a small area of private land within the Park where homesteaders occupied the land to establish their claims prior to the Park's creation in 1890	14.9
5.2	*Junction.* Road to Middle Fork Campground, about 50 sites maintained by the Forest Service as a part of the facilities	11.8
8.8	Park Boundary	8.2
9.0	Mather Ranger Station (H1)	8.0
10.5	Poopenaut Pass (H2)*	6.5
13.7	Poopenaut Valley viewpoint (H3)	3.3
16.6	Hetch Hetchy Reservoir (H4)	0.4
17.0	Hetch Hetchy Valley viewpoint (H5)	0.0

TIOGA ROAD (*Route 120 East*)

Driving along the Tioga Road you will pass through Yosemite's High Sierra, scenic country of lakes, meadows, domes, and ragged peaks. At 9,941 feet Tioga Pass crosses the crest of the Sierra Nevada, the highest automobile pass within the range and in the state of California. Often this high road is lined with snow even in July, and it may freeze any night of the year. Fresh snow falls and closes the road sometime between mid-October and mid-December, though a snowstorm may occur at any time. As a rule, the deep drifts on the Tioga Road cannot be plowed clear until late May or early June.

The original wagon road across Tioga Pass was constructed by the Great Sierra Consolidated Silver Company in 1883 to carry supplies to their operations on the east side of the range. Parts of that early road, in a slightly improved form, were used until 1961,

when the present-day Tioga Road through Yosemite National Park was completed. In several places within the Park, the old road can still be used to reach back-country lakes, streams, and campsites. Should you have the time, it is most interesting to take one of these crooked and narrow paved roadways to see how an earlier generation toured the Sierra Nevada. Inside the Park the new Tioga Road is easy driving, but outside it—especially the Lee Vining grade east of Tioga Pass—the roadway is steep and winding.

On Tioga Road, after leaving Crane Flat, you enter Gin Flat. This summit meadow is one of the locations within the Park where snow surveys are made during the winter to determine the amount of runoff that might be expected in the spring. This flat is supposed to have received its name when a barrel of gin bounced off a freight wagon and went unmissed by the driver. But, it was found by a group of road workers and sheepherders, who promptly got "gloriously ginned up."

Following a general northeasterly direction, the road proceeds through a pure stand of California red fir (see page 61). Along its route there are many western junipers. These trees are usually well twisted, but are sturdy enough to grow in Yosemite's exposed rocky places. At Siesta Lake, a little farther along, you can see how the low ridge of rocky debris across the road was built up as a terminal moraine of the cirque glacier from the ridge above and to the left of the lake. It acted as a dam, blocking the drainage of a small side stream, creating this little lake.

Past Siesta Lake and to the north, a spur follows the route of the Old Tioga Road about a mile to White Wolf, said to have been named after an Indian chieftain who frequently camped there. Facilities at White Wolf include a fine campground, meals, lodging, stables, ranger station, and naturalist activities during the summer season.

Just east of the White Wolf turnoff, a narrow, steep, and winding mountain road leaves the main route and leads four miles to Yosemite Creek and a small campground. This is a part of the Great Sierra Wagon Road, completed in 1883 for freighting machinery and supplies to the Tioga Mine, near Tioga Pass at the

Many beautiful lakes such as this one can be seen in High Sierra country from the Tioga Road. Around the shoreline of several of them are excellent examples of glacier polish, for the lake basins in this high-country region were excavated by moving ice. National Park Service photo

crest of the Sierra Nevada. Prior to 1961, a 21-mile section of this old road was the only route across Yosemite National Park and one of the few across the Sierra Nevada. Today you can take a side trip down the crooked lane to see how an earlier generation traveled.

The new Tioga Road, now proceeding in a generally easterly direction, crosses Yosemite Creek (this creek plunges 2,425 feet in Yosemite Valley as Yosemite Falls), proceeds to Porcupine Flat, a beautiful high mountain campground near Mount Hoffmann (10,850 feet). Crossing the May Lake Trail, and passing the road to Snow Flat, the road leads through spectacular landscapes to Tenaya Lake. Formed in a basin gouged by the Tenaya Branch of the Tuolumne Glacier, Tenaya Lake was named in honor of Chief Tenaya the leader of the Uzumate Indians. Tenaya Lake is surrounded by fine examples of glacier polish, for the lake basin was excavated by moving ice. At an elevation of 8,149 feet above sea level, it is one of the largest natural lakes in the Park, measuring a mile in length and a half mile in width. At the west end of the lake is a walk-in campground where visitors may park their cars and walk a short distance to attractive lakeside campsites. A picnic area is available at the east end.

Beyond Tenaya Lake, the road proceeds through "ghost forest" (a large number of dead trees killed by the lodgepole pine needleminer, a native insect), offers an excellent view of Mount Conness (12,590 feet), and then enters Tuolumne Meadows (8,594 feet). Available here during the summer season are a campground, Tuolumne Meadows Lodge, comfort stations, curio shop, grocery store, post office, restaurant, gas station, naturalist program, and ranger station. A short distance beyond the Tuolumne River crossing, roads lead to the north 0.5 mile to the carbonated Soda Springs and the Parsons Memorial Lodge of the Sierra Club, and to the south 1.5 miles to the Tuolumne Meadows High Sierra Camp. Actually Tuolumne Meadows is the main stop on the trail loop of 50 miles that is commonly referred to as the High Sierra Loop. There are six camps on the loop; in addition to Tuolumne Meadows Camp, there are Merced Lake Camp, Vogelsang Camp, Sunrise Camp, Glen Aulin Camp, and May Lake Camp. The camps are spaced about a day's hike (about 10 miles) apart and provide good food, lodging, and showers. See pages 102-107.

Tuolumne Meadows as viewed from Lembert Dome. National Park Service photo

One of the most interesting geological features of Tuolumne Meadows is Lembert Dome. Named for John Baptiste Lembert, goatherder, insect-collector, and homesteader in Tuolumne Meadows in 1885, this dome shows the sculpturing effect of ice. Its lopsided appearance was produced as glaciers pushed up the sloping east side and then tore chunks of rock off the west side, leaving it steepened. Patches of glistening glacier polish cover the face of the dome, and the top can be reached via a primitive path branching off the Dog Lake Trail. In the parking area near the dome's base is an interpretive sign that describes the formation of the jagged peaks around Tuolumne Meadows.

Continuing east from Tuolumne Meadows, the road soon crosses Tioga Pass (9,941 feet) on the boundary of Yosemite National Park. (Tioga is an Iroquois Indian word meaning "where it forks," and its use in Yosemite was perhaps inspired by a resident of Tioga County in New York.) This portion of the Park and Sierras is a most impressive high-mountain region, taking in meadows, lakes, timberline lodgepole pine forests, and 13,000-feet summits. Descending the rugged Lee Vining Canyon, the State Highway (Route 120) joins U. S. Highway 395 near Mono Lake (13.4 miles from Tioga Pass).

Miles	*Points of Interest*	*Miles*
0.0	*Junction.* Big Oak Flat Road (Route 120 West)	45.6
0.2	Crane Flat viewpoint (T1)	45.4
3.2	*Junction* (T2). Old Big Oak Flat Road to Tamarack Flat Campground. Road continues 6.1 miles to Gentry's, a point where the road at one time began its descent into Yosemite Valley via a series of switchbacks	42.4
3.3	Gin Flat viewpoint (T3)	42.3
4.3	Walker Party site (T4). An interpretive sign here describes the travels of the Joseph R. Walker party, the first white men to enter the Yosemite region	41.3
6.9	South Fork of the Tuolumne River crossing (T5)	38.7
8.7	*Junction* (T6). Road to Smoky Jack Campground	36.9
10.0	California red pine forest (T7)	35.6
13.0	Siesta Lake viewpoint (T8)	32.6
13.9	*Junction* (T9). Old Tioga Road to White Wolf Lodge, White Wolf and Harden Lake Campgrounds, ranger station, and other limited visitor services	31.7

Miles	*Points of Interest*	*Miles*
14.2	*Junction* (T10). Old Tioga Road to Yosemite Creek Campground (6.0 miles)	31.4
16.0	Clark Range viewpoint (T11). An identifier points out the peaks seen from this spot. Mount Clark and the Clark Range were named for Galen Clark, the first guardian of the Yosemite Grant	29.6
17.4	Western juniper—near post T12	28.2
17.6	Yosemite Creek viewpoint (T13)	28.0
17.7	Example of exfoliating granite (T14)*—see page 39	27.9
19.0	Yosemite Creek crossing (T15)	26.6
19.4	Quaking aspen (T16)—an interpretive sign describes the traits of this tree	26.2
23.0	*Junction* (T17). Road to Porcupine Flat Campground	22.6
23.6	Cone-bearing Trees Nature Trail (T18). Signs along this trail point out and describe five of the commonest trees along the Tioga Road (Jeffrey pine, western white pine, lodgepole pine, white fir, and California red fir)	22.0
24.1	*Junction* (T19). Road to Porcupine Creek Campground. Trail to North Dome (3.7 miles) starts at campground	21.5
24.9	Half Dome viewpoint (T20)	20.7
26.2	*Junction* (T21). May Lake Road. At 1.8 mile point on this road, the trail to May Lake High Sierra Camp begins. The May Lake Road leads through Snow Flat, where winter snow surveys are made. Interpretive sign here explains the story of snow in the Sierra Nevada	19.4
26.6	Glacial moraine (T22) deposited by the Tuolumne Glacier is evident in this road-cut	19.0
27.0	Clouds Rest viewpoint (T23)	18.6
28.4	Olmsted Point parking area (T24). Three interpretive signs describe the scenic and geological features, and a $\frac{1}{4}$-mile trail leads to a nearby dome for fine views down Tenaya Canyon to Half Dome and up the canyon to Tenaya Lake	17.2
30.2	Tenaya Lake parking area (T25) for walk-in campsite	15.4

(Continued)

(*Continued from page 61*).

Miles	Points of Interest	Miles
31.4	Tenaya Lake day-use area (picnic sites)	14.2
32.9	Ghost Forest interpretive sign (T26)	12.7
34.0	Mount Conness viewpoint (T27)	11.6
35.1	Fairview Dome—south of post T28	10.5
36.3	Tuolumne Meadows interpretive sign (T29)	9.3
38.5	*Junction* (T30). Roads to visitor facilities: Tuolumne Meadows Campground, restrooms, curio shop, gas station, grocery store, restaurant, post office, Tuolumne Meadow Lodge, and ranger station	7.1
38.6	Tuolumne River crossing (T31)	7.0
38.7	*Junction* (T32). Roads to Soda Springs and Parsons Memorial Lodge (0.5 mile north) and Tuolumne Meadows Camp (1.5 miles south)	6.9
39.6	Dog Lake Trail parking area and Lembert Dome interpretive sign	6.0
40.3	Glacial moraine (T33) exposed in this road-cut was left by Lyell Glacier, one of the Park's few remaining glaciers	5.3
40.9	Dana Fork of the Tuolumne River crossing (T34)	4.7
42.8	Mono Trail interpretive sign (T35) describes the old Indian trail over Mono Pass and outlines the prominent peaks	2.8
43.8	Mount Dana—Mount Gibbs viewpoint (T36)	1.8
44.2	Lodgepole pine forest (T37)	1.4
45.4	Dana Meadows viewpoint (T38). Interpretive sign here explains the story of the development of Dana Meadows	0.2
45.5	Tioga Pass Entrance Station	0.1
45.6	Tioga Pass (T39) and Park Boundary	0.0

WAWONA OR FRESNO ROAD (*Route 41*)

This road follows fairly closely the route taken by the Mariposa Battalion when in 1851 they became the first white men to enter Yosemite Valley. The original Wawona Road was built in 1875, and until 1933 when the present road replaced it, visitors first saw Yosemite Valley from Inspiration Point on the old road, higher on the slope above. Today its place has been taken by Tunnel View, a superior panoramic and photogenic overlook at the east end of Wawona Tunnel. An interpretive sign here outlines the valley's profile and identifies landmarks. If you wish to go to Inspiration Point, take the 1¼-mile self-guiding nature trail that begins at the upper parking area. Guide booklets are available at the trail start in summer and at the Yosemite Valley Visitor Center during other periods.

The Wawona Tunnel, 0.8 mile in length, is the longest of the four in the Park. (The other three are on the Big Oak Flat Road.) It was blasted out of granite to avoid a road-cut that would have seriously defaced the landscape. Drilled entirely from the lower east side, it was completed in 1933, after two and a half years of hazardous work with no serious injury. Some 81,113 cubic yards of solid rock had to be removed. Ventilating fans in the tunnel come on automatically when needed to eliminate automobile fumes.

The road between the Tunnel and Chinquapin offers several magnificent views of the lower Merced Canyon and, on clear days, of the San Joaquin Valley and Coast Range, about 100 miles away. Just after leaving the Tunnel, the road passes through a granite slab composed of thin curved layers or shells of rock. Through the erosional process of exfoliation by load relief the rock has expanded and broken parallel to the surface.

Chinquapin Junction receives its name from an evergreen shrub common here. It is a brush about four feet high and has leaves with green upper surfaces and yellow under surfaces. Related to the American chestnut, it bears a burrlike fruit, and grows in the Sierra Nevada on warm open slopes at elevations from 3,000 to 8,000 feet. The Chinquapin Junction which is at 6,040 feet, has been an important intersection since the 1850's and today is the turnoff for Glacier Point. The service station at the junction operates during the day most of the year.

Continuing along the Wawona Road beyond Chinquapin, you will come to a junction with the Henness Ridge road. About one mile down this graded road along the top of Henness Ridge is a fire lookout, on one of the highest points. It is manned throughout the fire danger period, usually from mid-June to mid-October, and visitors are welcome. There you can see that along the top of Henness Ridge was once a logging railway. Locomotives hauled loaded log cars over 25 miles of track from private lands within the Park to a steep incline track laid straight down the mountain about one mile to the west. There the cars were lowered to the Yosemite Valley Railroad in the bottom of the Merced Canyon at El Portal, and as they descended their weight was used to pull unloaded cars back up the grade. This operation was conducted between 1912 and 1924 by the Yosemite Lumber Company, but since then their woodlands have been acquired by the government and are now returning to a natural state as National Park lands. Incidentally, the name "Henness" apparently is a shortened version of Hennessy, an old-time resident who built a trail near here.

A little farther along, the road crosses Rail Creek. During winters of heavy snow, skiers follow a trail from the Badger Pass ski area to this spot. Approximately 2 miles long, it is a steep, narrow path and should only be attempted by experts. The stream here is officially known as Elevenmile Creek because a stagecoach station was once located near it, but its local name is Rail Creek, after Rail Meadows where split rails for fences were once obtained.

The road then winds through stately forests of sugar pine, Jeffrey pine, and red and white fir, and descends into the valley of the South Fork of the Merced at Wawona. Named for an Indian word that may have meant "big tree," Wawona was originally a trailside tourist camp operated by Galen Clark. He built a cabin known as Clark's Station which provided an overnight stopping-place for visitors enroute between Yosemite Valley and the Mariposa Grove of Giant Sequoias (Big Trees). When the Wawona Road to Yosemite Valley was being built in 1875, the Washburn brothers purchased Clark's station and built most of the buildings of the Wawona Hotel, now under the management of the Yosemite Park and Curry Co. Facilities in the area that are available during the heavier travel periods include stores, meals, cabins, trailer park, service station, hotel, stables, and golf course.

The Wawona Campground, originally named Camp A. E. Wood after Captain Wood, the first acting military superintendent of Yosemite National Park, this site was used by the U.S. Army as its principal camp and administration headquarters from 1891 to 1906. Also, at Wawona, on both sides of and actually spanning the South Fork of the Merced River is the Pioneer Yosemite History Center, a collection of furnished cabins and buildings, an old jail, horse-drawn vehicles, exhibits, and a covered bridge. A visit will give you a glimpse into the horse era of Yosemite's past, over 100 years ago.

From Wawona the road climbs to the South Entrance of the Park and then continues on to Fresno.

Miles	Points of Interest	Miles
0.0	*Junction*. Yosemite Village Loop Road (South Road)	26.3
0.1	Bridalveil Fall parking area (W1). Trail 0.2 mile to observation point near base of Fall	26.2
1.6	Tunnel viewpoint (W2)	24.7
1.7	Wawona Tunnel portal	24.6
2.5	Wawona Tunnel portal	23.8
3.3	Turtleback Dome viewpoint (W3)	23.0
4.5	Coulterville Road viewpoint (W4). The old wagon road can be seen descending the partly wooded rocky slope across the Merced Canyon. Also Elephant Rock (which looks somewhat like its namesake) is farther west along the rim of the canyon	21.8
9.3	*Chinquapin Junction* (W5). Intersection with Glacier Point Road. Also service station	17.0
9.8	*Junction* (W6). Road to Henness Ridge fire lookout	16.5
11.2	Rail Creek crossing (W7)	15.1
20.5	*Junction*. Road to Wawona Campground (W8)	5.8
21.3	*Junction*. Road to Pioneer Yosemite History Center	5.0
21.4	South Fork of the Merced River crossing (W9)	4.9
21.5	*Junction* (W10). Road to Pioneer Yosemite History Center. Post office, grocery store, cafe, gas station	4.8
21.6	*Junction*. Road (east) to Wawona Hotel. Chowchilla Mountain Road (to Merced) and Wawona Loop Road (east)	4.7
21.8	*Junction* (W11). Wawona Meadow Loop Road (Do not enter here.) Also Wawona Meadow viewpoint	4.5
26.2	*Junction*. Mariposa Grove Road. Also South Entrance Station (W12) and restrooms	0.1
26.3	Park Boundary	0.0

GLACIER POINT ROAD

The present Glacier Point Road was completed in 1936, replacing the original wagon path constructed in 1882. In several places the route of the old road may still be seen, and in others the new roadway follows the alignment of the old. The road starts at Chinquapin Junction and climbs easterly through beautiful stands of pine and fir by way of the Badger Pass ski area and Bridalveil

Creek. There are several interesting viewpoints along the way such as the one at Clark Range. Mount Clark itself is the higher peak at the north (left) end of the range standing 11,522 feet high. It can be easily identified by the avalanche track on its face, a barren area extending into the forest below the peak where snowslides rip through the trees in winter and spring. The most prominent of the domed peaks between you and the Clark Range is Mount Starr King, named in honor of a Unitarian pastor whose writings in 1860 called attention to the wonders of Yosemite. (Another fine view of the Clark Range can be obtained at Washburn Point, a little along on this road.) The low ridge on the horizon far to the south (right) is Horse Ridge, its highest point at about 9,500 feet. It is popular as a back-country ski area because snow melts slowly on the shaded north side of the ridge—the side seen from the road—and often remains there when the adjacent country is clear. Below the ridge and out of sight is Ostrander Lake, on the shore of which is a ski hut. During snowy winter months, reservations may be made for lodging and meals at the hut, which can be reached at that time by ski or snowshoe trips or on over-snow vehicles from Badger Pass (see pages 166-170). In summer the hut is closed but the area is open to anglers and hikers.

As you continue toward Glacier Point, the road passes through such interesting uplands as Monroe Meadows (named in honor of a Negro stage driver), Peregoy Meadow (named for Charles E. Peregoy, early hotel operator), and Pothole Meadows. Odd round pools of water about five feet in diameter form in bowl-shaped depressions in the Pothole Meadows during the wet months of spring and early summer.

After leaving the meadowlands, you come to a side road which leads to Sentinel Dome. At the base of the Dome autos are parked for a short hike to its top. Here an extensive view meets the eye: Mount Hoffman, Basket and North Domes, Cloud's Rest and Half Dome, Nevada and Vernal Falls and Mount Starr King; the mountains of the Tuolumne Pass region, Mount Maclure, Mount Lyell, and Mount Florence, and the peaks of the Merced Range ring the horizon beyond. El Capitan and Cathedral Rocks, and much of the lower end of the Valley are seen to the west. On Sentinel Dome's summit, itself, stands one of the most photographed trees in the

The High Sierra as seen from Glacier Point. Liberty Cap (left), Nevada Fall (right), while Vernal Fall is at bottom. National Park Service photo

world—a gnarled and wind-shaped Jeffrey pine—which grows here in solid rock. An interesting group of granite boulders deposited by glaciers can be seen at the base of the Dome near the parking area.

As you continue on the Glacier Point Road you cross Illilouette Ridge and come to Washburn Point. At this point you have an excellent view into the gorge of the Merced River. If you listen carefully, the roar of Nevada and Vernal Falls as they drop down the Giant's Stairway can be heard. Less than a mile from Washburn Point, you reach Glacier Point.

Actually, a walk of about 300 yards from the parking area takes you to Glacier Point, which is beyond and to the left of the hotel. From this famous viewpoint, 3,250 feet above the floor of Yosemite Valley, the eye looks eastward over a vast panorama of forest, lakes, deep canyons, waterfalls, and high peaks of Yosemite's High Sierra—a part of the longest, the highest, and grandest single mountain range in the United States. Glacier Point also offers very interesting bird's-eye views of the floor and north walls of the Valley, and of the uplands above it. The rock formations of this grand view are identified by the interpretive sign below the Glacier Point Overlook Museum. Inside the museum exhibits explain how the peaks, canyons, domes, and falls were formed. While this point was once covered by over 700 feet of ice, the origin of the name *Glacier Point* is obscure, for no one had visualized such an extensive glacier when the name was first recorded in 1868, and no glaciers can be seen from the point. (The white patches of snow often visible in the distance in spring and summer melt before the next winter's snow falls.) A naturalist is on duty nearly every day in the summer to help visitors understand the scene, and to present scheduled campfire programs in the evenings.

Facilities at Glacier Point during the summer season include a hotel, cafeteria, gift shop, restrooms, campground and naturalist programs. The building housing the cafeteria is called the Mountain House, and was constructed in 1878 for James McCauley, making it the oldest building in the Park still in use. The hotel dates back to 1917, when it was constructed by the Desmond Company. Today both facilities are operated by a single concessioner, the Yosemite Park and Curry Co. Lodging and meals may be obtained here even during the winter, for a manager remains throughout the snowy months to protect the buildings, produce the firefall, and to feed and shelter ambitious skiers and snowshoers who have given advance notice of their arrival. The Glacier Point Road is closed beyond Badger Pass Ski Center junction during the winter months.

Miles	Points of Interest	Miles
0.0	*Chinquapin Junction.* Wawona Road (Route 41)	15.4
1.9	Merced Canyon viewpoint (G1)	13.5
4.9	*Junction* (G2). Road to Badger Pass Ski Center. Monroe Meadows	10.5
7.2	Merced Peak viewpoint (G3)	8.2
7.6	*Junction* (G4). Road to Bridalveil Creek Campground. Peregoy Meadow	7.8
8.1	Bridalveil Creek crossing (G5)	7.3
10.6	Clark Range and Horse Ridge viewpoint (G6)	4.8
12.8	Pothole Meadows (G7)	2.6
13.0	Sentinel Dome view (G8)*	2.4
13.6	Switchbacks (G9)*. Start of steep portion of road	1.8
13.9	*Junction.* Road to Sentinel Dome trail (0.5 mile)	1.5
14.6	Washburn Point parking area (G10)	0.8
15.4	Glacier Point parking area (G11). Mountain House and Glacier Point Hotel—cafeteria, gift shop, restrooms, Glacier Point Campground. Location of Firefall (see page 175)	0.0

MARIPOSA GROVE ROAD

The Mariposa Grove contains about 500 mature Giant Sequoias and spreads over 250 acres at elevations ranging from 5,500 to nearly 7,000 feet. It could really be considered as two groves within one, for there is a lower section containing the huge Grizzly Giant and an upper one in which a 2-mile loop drive passes through the famous Wawona Tunnel Tree and leads to a scenic overlook at Wawona Point. Both sections are open nearly all year, but following snowstorms in winter the lower grove may be closed temporarily, while the upper tunnel loop road is sometimes closed for several weeks at a time. Trailers must be left in the parking area at the South Entrance at all times.

The huge reddish-brown-trunked Giant Sequoias standing on either side of the road mark the entrance to the Mariposa Grove. This stand was probably discovered by Major Burney, the first sheriff of Mariposa County, and John McCauley in 1849. By 1857, Galen Clark was known to have explored it thoroughly, named it, and helped bring it to public attention.

Meanwhile, an incident involving the de-barking of a large Giant Sequoia in the Calaveras Grove (north of Yosemite) had raised a public outcry and fanned an interest in preserving a grove of the trees intact. The bark from the stripped tree had been shipped east and then to London as an exhibit to lure travelers to California, but back home the tree died. So it was that in 1864 the Mariposa Grove was set apart along with Yosemite Valley as the world's first public preserve of this kind and Galen Clark was appointed its first Guardian. (You can see the site of his cabin near the present Mariposa Grove Museum.) In 1890 the land between Yosemite Valley and the Mariposa Grove was made a National Park and in 1906 the Valley and the Grove were included.

A naturalist is on duty at Mariposa Grove (Big Trees) Museum and gives talks on the trees. Near the museum is the fallen Massachusetts Tree, an immense sequoia, 280 feet long and 28 feet in diameter, that was blown over in the winter of 1927. As the tree is broken into several sections, it provides an excellent opportunity to study the rings and the character of the wood. In August 1934 another giant, the Stable Tree fell. It is located just above the museum. But the most famous of the downed trees is the "Fallen Monarch." Once a majestic standing giant, the massive trunk lying alongside the road long ago succumbed to gravity. The date of its fall is unknown, for there is no record even in Indian legend of a time when it was upright. Through the years its bark has fallen off and disintegrated, but its heartwood of high tannin concentration endures and will most likely last for many decades more.

Across the road from the Fallen Monarch, a walk of about 100 yards up an old stagecoach road leads to the Corridor Tree, indicated by the sign. Through the centuries fires have eaten nearly through its massive trunk, and now only six columns of sapwood and a central shaft of heartwood support the tree and provide the foliage with minerals and water from the roots in the earth far below. Even so, the tree seems healthy and is producing new bark and new layers of wood.

The Clothespin Tree is another fine example of the sequoia's durability. Named because it is shaped like an old-fashioned clothespin, the opening is about 40 feet high and 15 feet across at the base, tapering upward. Repeated fires have burned out its center, but the thickness and porosity of the bark provided enough insulation from the heat of the burning forest to save the growing tissues. It still stands, although its support has largely been removed. Similar scars, though less dramatic, are on most of the large sequoias, indicating that fire has long been a part of this species' environment. Of course, fire damage to a sequoia trunk can prevent sap from flowing to the top of the tree, causing it to die.

70

The Grizzly Giant is the largest tree in the grove with a base diameter of 30 feet, girth of 94.2 feet and height of 200 feet. There is no accurate way of knowing the age of the Grizzly Giant but its size and gnarled appearance indicate that it is at least 3,800 years old and probably more. No trees known are larger or older than the *Sequoia gigantea*. See Chapter 5 for details.

SIZE OF BIG TREES IN MARIPOSA GROVE

Name of the trees	Girth at base	Diameter at base	Height
	Feet	Feet	Feet
Grizzly Giant	94.2	30.0	200
Faithful Couple	95.8	30.5	244
Columbia	88.1	28.0	290
La Fayette	96.1	30.6	267
General Sheridan	78.0	24.8	259
St. Louis	78.6	25.0	277
Wawona	86.4	27.5	231
Washington	93.5	29.7	238
Mark Twain	55.7	17.7	274
Virginia	89.3	28.4	186
Clothespin	69.6	22.2	293
California	78.1	22.8	234
Lincoln	72.0	22.9	258
General Logan	76.0	24.2	259
South Carolina	74.0	23.5	246

The Big Trees Lodge, which is situated right in the heart of the Mariposa Grove, is open from mid-May to early October to care for those who wish to spend a day or so among these giants of the forest (see page 184). Cafeteria-style meals are available.

If your vehicle is much wider or higher than a normal passenger car, do not drive beyond the museum, for the road narrows and then passes through a tree via an irregularly shaped hole about 8 feed wide and 9 feet high. You may park at the museum and take the ¼-mile trail that leads up to the Wawona Tunnel Tree. In 1881 the Yosemite Stage and Turnpike Company paid the Scribner brothers $75 to enlarge an old burn scar to the present tunnel size of 8 feet wide, 9 feet high, and 26 feet long. The tree itself is 20 feet through above the root swell and 234 feet high. Cutting holes through giant sequoias is not practiced by the National Park Service, but this tree is still growing well despite its handicap.

Miles	Points of Interest	Miles
0.0	*Junction.* Wawona Road (Route 4). South Entrance Station	6.1
1.9	Entrance to Mariposa Grove (S1)	4.2
2.0	Mariposa Grove Ranger Station (S2)	4.1
2.1	The Fallen Monarch and Corridor Tree (S3)	4.0
2.9	Grizzly Giant (S4)—largest tree in Yosemite	3.2
3.8	Clothespin Tree (S5)	2.3
4.4	Young sequoias—directly behind post S6	1.7
4.6	Mariposa Grove Museum (S7). Also Big Tree Lodge	1.5
5.4	Wawona Tunnel Tree (S8)	0.7
6.1	Wawona Point (S9)	0.0

MOTOR TOURS IN THE PARK

While all these drives may be enjoyed with your own automobile, the Yosemite Transportation System operates comfortable motor coaches and limousines. Many families that drive to the Park in their cars, board buses for the various conducted tours. The drivers, besides being experienced, are well-versed in the history and lore of Yosemite. They thus make thoroughly competent guides, whose knowledge and experience add much to the journeys along these historic roads. The following are the major motor tours in the Park:

Mariposa Grove of Big Trees, a daily drive from Yosemite Valley accommodations to the Mariposa Grove of Big Trees. During the winter season, trip is operated to Grizzly Giant only, but side trip to Badger Pass Ski House is included in lieu of complete tour of Grove.

Glacier Point, a half-day drive from Yosemite Valley accommodation to Glacier Point. Operates from approximately June 1 to November 30.

Loop Trip, combination all-day tour of Mariposa Grove of Big Trees and Glacier Point. Operates from approximately June 1 to November 30.

Yosemite Valley, a daily, year-around, 2-hour drive, viewing principal points of interest which are identified and described by a driver-escort.

Other motor trips are available to White Wolf, Tuolumne Meadows, and Hetch Hetchy by special arrangements. All trips start from and return to The Ahwahnee, Camp Curry, and Yosemite Lodge. Schedules, fare rates, and other information may be obtained from the transportation desks of these establishments.

PHOTOGRAPHY IN THE PARK

Yosemite National Park is an ideal setting for the photographer. But, there are a few things to remember while taking pictures in the Park. Few amateurs, for instance, realize what an important part light and shade play in the composition of photographs. Under the high noonday sun most pictures are "flat" and lifeless, and it is during the morning and afternoon hours that you will *generally* get your best exposures. Strong side-lighting is also best for good photographs of Yosemite's natural features. Side-lighting gives a bold, sculptural feeling of third-dimensional relief, plus maximum texture. There are exceptions, of course; Half Dome in silhouette is equally beautiful. But, remember that no matter how beautiful a subject is at a given time, it is most beautiful at some certain hours during the day.

Subject	Best Time	Subject	Best Time
Mirror Lake	8 to 9 A.M.	El Capitan	Early morning and around 1.30 P.M.
Vernal Fall	10 A.M. to Noon		
Nevada Fall	11 A.M. to 1 P.M.		
Bridalveil Fall	1 to 3 P.M.	Yosemite Falls	Mid-morning and 1 to 2.30 P.M.
Big Trees	Early morning and late afternoon		
		Tunnel View	2 to 4 P.M.
Half Dome	2:30 to 3.30 P.M.	North Dome	10 to 11 A.M.
Valley View	2 to 4 P.M.	Happy Isles	10 A.M. to Noon

The foregoing remarks are but a few of the many which might be included if space permitted. The various photographic suppliers in the Park (see page 198) will be pleased to make further suggestions to those who consult them in Yosemite National Park.

Chapter 4.

Trails of the Park

FROM THE Park's road system a vast panorama of scenery is revealed, and with luck some wildlife also may be observed, particularly during the early morning and evening. For a more intimate contact and to fully appreciate this wonderful region, the Park's 700 miles of well-marked and well-maintained trails offer many new and interesting experiences. Actually, the scenery of the "back country" is a living museum of nature.

BACK-PACKING IN THE PARK

Back-pack hiking is the most economical way to get into the back country. It is rather strenuous, but there are certain definite advantages of this means of reaching and enjoying the more remote areas of the Park. You can be entirely independent and self-sufficient. You can camp in otherwise inaccessible places with no worry about horse feed or strayed burros.

Back-packing requires careful planning. You must get down to bare essentials and scrutinize everything that goes into your pack for weight and bulk. A pack that is too heavy can spoil any trip, as can a pack without a sufficiently warm sleeping bag, or lack of adequate food or clothing. Replenish your food supply at the High Sierra Camps and sleep out under the clear Sierra skies; drink the icy waters of remote streams and lakes, and smell frying bacon and fragrant coffee over a campfire.

74

Family hikers look down into Yosemite Valley from Dewey Point.
Courtesy of Edgar T. Menning

Sleeping Equipment. A good lightweight down, feather, orlon, kapok, or wool sleeping bag, 3 to 6 pounds. There are new-type bags which reduce weight and bulk, yet provide warmth. On cold nights wear socks, sweater, etc. In addition to the above, a poncho, slicker, or lightweight waterproofed material, such as light canvas or even a shower curtain, should be carried. Some may want a three-quarter length air mattress, weight 4 pounds, but most people can sleep quite well on pine needles.

Clothing. Sturdy, well broken-in, leather shoes (high boots not necessary) with composition soles, or ankle-high tennis or basket-ball shoes. An extra wool shirt or a sweater is necessary for cool nights in higher elevations. We suggest wearing 2 pairs of socks to protect feet from friction. One pair need not be wool. Change socks every night, wash dirty ones and pin them outside of pack to dry next day. Carry in your pack 1 extra shirt, 1 change of underwear, toilet articles. Avoid short sleeves and shorts. Wear a hat with a brim. Blue jeans are good.

Cooking Equipment. 1 frying pan with collapsible handle. Tin cans can serve as utensils, or 2 small aluminum nesting pots or cans with wire handles. 1 small coffee pot is convenient. Boy Scout or Army mess kits are useful for back-packing.

Food. Dehydrated foods are preferred by the back-packer. These include soups, eggs, milk, fruits, and vegetables. A prepared flour for pancakes, biscuits, dumplings is suggested. A small compact head of cabbage and a few well-selected onions are worth their weight. Plan every meal before your trip and pack accordingly. Use small cloth sacks for light weight and compactness.

Yosemite Park and Curry Co. has a limited line of food supplies for sale at the High Sierra Camps (see page 187). Hikers should bring their own containers. Tuolumne Meadows store, the Wawona store, Camp Curry store, and stores in the Village, Camp 14, and Housekeeping Camp carry a complete line of groceries.

Miscellaneous Equipment. Small first-aid kit containing adhesive tape, gauze, Merthiolate, lip pomade, sunburn and mosquito lotions, sun glasses, topographic map obtainable from the Yosemite Visitor Center (see page 44), and a book on camp cooking, hiking, and trail sense. Carry a good knife, candle, compact snakebite kit, flashlight, matches in waterproof case, small scissors, safety pins. A hand axe is too heavy in comparison to its usefulness. Use a good lightweight rucksack or packboard.

Fire Precautions. Great care is necessary to guard against fire. *See a Park Ranger before you start on your trip and secure fire permit.* You can benefit by the ranger's knowledge and experience as to the best places to camp and the most important points of interest. Always soak down campfire and see that the coals are cold the full depth before leaving. Smoke only in a clear place, and *never* while on the trail. Be sure cigarettes and matches are completely extinguished before moving on.

When hiking start slowly and keep a moderate pace. It is never wise to travel alone; but if you must, stick to the frequently used trails in case you become sick or injured. Even groups should always leave word where they are going and when they expect to return. The slogan "Be Careful" is just as appropriate in Yosemite's back country as on the streets. Also take care of your health. A normally minor illness can become serious in the high elevations; a head cold can quickly turn to pneumonia. If you become ill, try to get out of the mountains, or at least to a lower elevation, while you can still travel. A summer rarely passes without several people becoming seriously ill or injured in the back country. This not only ruins the trip for the person and his companions, but it is expensive. The Park does not own a helicopter, but can arrange for one in serious emergencies when evacuation is impossible by other means. Commercial helicopters are usually available—at $130 or more an hour—and the costs must be borne by the group or individual. Military helicopters are available for life or death emergencies, but because of distances they cannot always be obtained in time.

When you think you are lost, keep calm. If you told your companions where you were going someone will soon be looking for you. But, in the meantime, do the following:

1. Sit down. Try to figure out where you are. Use your head, not your legs. Do not panic.

2. At night, in fog or storm, stop at once and make camp in a sheltered place. Gather plenty of dry fuel and build a fire in a safe place. (Put it out when you leave.)

3. Three of anything—shouts, smokes, fires, etc.—is a sign of distress. If seen or heard help will soon be on the way.

Be prepared for the weather. Summer weather in the High Sierra is remarkably pleasant by mountain standards. You should, however, have a lightweight ground cloth or some plastic that can be rigged for a tent if it should rain. Daytime temperatures are often in the upper seventies, but the nights are cold, occasionally down to freezing and below.

SADDLE TRIPS IN THE PARK

A horseback ride around Yosemite Valley, or anywhere in the Park, is a rewarding experience. For not only is there the enjoyment of riding a well-mannered horse, but also one has a chance to see byways not accessible from the roads. There are stables located in the Valley, at Tuolumne Meadows, Wawona, Mather, and at White Wolf. At the Valley stables there is a most comprehensive program with guided trips or rides off the Valley floor.

At Wawona there are pleasant trails around the meadow or up into higher mountain country, or, upon arrangement, to the Mariposa Grove of Big Trees.

From Tuolumne, there are fine day rides, with fishing lakes as destinations, or, equally enjoyable, are rides simply to see the wonderful country on every side.

The Mather stable is in the northwest part of the Park and there are well-marked trails to Smith Meadows and the Tuolumne River Basin.

From White Wolf stable, Harden and Luken Lakes, the Ten Lakes Basin, and the Grand Canyon of the Tuolumne are accessible. Each stable is equipped to provide comprehensive service and the personnel at each is familiar with the trails and lakes.

Where one wishes to go will determine from which stable he should start his trip. For those preferring to do a minimum of camp "chores," guides, cooks (with food), and wranglers will make the trip and camp-living most comfortable. Or, if the "do-it-yourself" urge compels you to be self-sufficient, pack burros and mules are available to carry camp gear. (Here your party does the walking, with a burro carrying your gear. This makes it possible for families with small children, or those who cannot carry the loads required in back-packing, to enjoy the wilderness at a minimum of cost.) And, anywhere in between, you can have just the sort of service you desire. One particularly popular service is "spot-packing" in which the party with its gear is packed to a pre-determined location and later picked up for the return trip. Independent parties should secure fire permits from the National Park Service office. On guided trips, the guide takes care of the permit. Arrangements and rates covering any of the above can be had at Yosemite Park and Curry Co. offices (see page 181). There also are some packers holding permits to operate in Yosemite National Park along the east, west, and south boundaries of the Park. A list of these outfits or packers may be obtained through the Superintendent's office (see page 11).

With a "do-it-yourself" arrangement, you do your own packing and are responsible for the welfare of the animals. The packer you rent from will help you get started and then you are on your own. The load limit on burros is generally 75 pounds, and 150 pounds for a mule. Lightweight equipment, and at least partial use of dehydrated foods will enable you to get by with fewer animals.

There are group trips available in the Park and some of these are described on pages 107-108.

TRAILS OF THE PARK

Yosemite Valley is completely encircled with bridle paths. They stem from the Yosemite Park and Curry Co. stables, as all riding trips start and end there. The paths are usually at no great distance from the Valley roads. The road and bridle path mileages are approximately the same (see pages 82-101). Leisurely riding time is approximately three miles per hour, so the time necessary to transverse these paths can be easily calculated. While the horses are well trained and know the terrain, it is not advisable to ride alone unless you are an experienced rider, familiar with the Valley. Guided parties are scheduled regularly during the spring, summer, and fall, with special Western breakfasts, and trips arranged especially for young people. The transportation desk at the Ahwahnee, Camp Curry, or Yosemite Lodge, as well as the wranglers at the stables, will be glad to give necessary information or make reservations.

Horses must be kept on the trails or bridle paths in the Valley at all times. No horses are permitted off the floor of the Valley without an authorized guide. The grades of all trails leading from the Valley except a few steep foot trails (Sierra Point Trail and Mist Trail) have been carefully considered with regard to the rider and hiker. On all trails in the Park, horses and mules have the right-of-way. This applies also to motorists on the roads, who must always permit saddle and pack-animals to pass. In permitting a rider to pass, a hiker should stand very still, off the trail on the downhill side.

The sign-system of the Yosemite trails is most efficient and complete, with easy visibility and accurate mileages. The following are some of the more popular trails. As you will note, it is possible to start many of these trails at various places and make shorter loop trips. By studying the various routes given in the following pages, road mileage tables (see Chapter 3), and with the assistance of a topographic map, you can make up a proposed back-country trip. Show your plans to the District Ranger and ask for his suggestions and comments. There are six Ranger Districts in Yosemite National Park:

District No. 1, Yosemite Valley, Headquarters, Administration Building.

District No. 2, Northwest Section of Park, Headquarters, Mather Ranger Station (substation at Hetch Hetchy).

District No. 3, Northeast and Eastern areas, Headquarters, Tuolumne Meadows Ranger Station.

District No. 4, Southern area, Headquarters, Wawona Ranger Station.

District No. 5, Glacier Point, Badger Pass ski area, Headquarters, Chinquapin Ranger Station.

District No. 6, Central area, Headquarters, Crane Flat Ranger Station.

Riders on the Long (Eleven-Mile) Trail to Glacier Point. Note Nevada Fall and Liberty Cap in the background. Yosemite Park and Curry Co. photo

In the following tables mileages are given from one point of interest or junction of trails. A mountain hiker can usually cover three miles of ordinary trail or ascend 1,000 feet of average graded terrain per hour. Hence, for example, allow about three hours for a hike to Glacier Point via Four-Mile Trail (often called the Short Trail), and about five hours to top of Half Dome from Happy Isles.

YOSEMITE TRAILS

YOSEMITE TO GLACIER POINT VIA VERNAL AND NEVADA FALLS, ELEVEN MILE (LONG) TRAIL, AND RETURN BY SHORT (FOUR MILE) TRAIL—15.6 MILES

Name	Distance between points	Elevation above sea level	Remarks
Yosemite Visitors Center		3,970	
Happy Isles (junction Nevada Falls Trail)	2.4	4,034	Beautiful river scenery
Junction Mist Trail	1.0	4,550	Foot trail to top Vernal Falls
Junction Merced Lake Trail	2.2	5,950	Trail branches to Merced Lake and Tuolumne Meadows
Top Nevada Falls	.2	5,970	Beautiful view from top of falls
Panorama Cliff	2.2	6,224	Beautiful view of Merced Canyon
Illilouette Falls	.6	5,825	Height of falls, 370 feet
Junction Buena Vista Trail	.6	6,400	Trail to Johnson Lake and Buck Camp
Glacier Point	1.5	7,214	Hotel and camp accommodations. Beautiful view of Yosemite Valley and High Sierra
Floor Valley (foot Glacier Point Short Trail)	3.5	4,000	
Yosemite Visitors Center	1.4	3,970	

Yosemite to Glacier Point via Short Trail and Return via Pohono Trail and Inspiration Point on Wawona Road—23.4 Miles

Name	Distance between points	Elevation above sea level	Remarks
Yosemite Visitor Center		3,970	
Foot of Short Trail	1.4	4,000	
Union Point	2.2	6,314	Beautiful view of Yosemite Valley
Glacier Point	1.3	7,214	Hotel and camp accommodations. Beautiful view of Yosemite Valley and High Sierra
Junction Sentinel Dome Trail	0.6	7,600	Sentinel Dome 0.5 mile west. Beautiful view of High Sierra
Junction Pohono Trail and Glacier Point Road	1.0	7,725	
Taft Point and The Fissures	1.1	7,503	Beautiful view of Yosemite Valley. Fissures are several hundred feet deep
Bridalveil Creek	2.1	6,700	Good fishing
Junction Pohono and Alder Creek Trails	0.2	7,000	Trail branches to Wawona
Dewey Point	2.2	7,316	Beautiful view of Yosemite Valley
Crocker Point	0.6	7,090	Same as above
Stanford Point	0.6	6,659	Same as above
Old Inspiration Point	0.8	6,603	Same as above
Inspiration Point	1.9	5,391	Beautiful view of Yosemite Valley. From this point on is Old Indian trail Yosemite, discovered in 1851
Floor Valley (Pohono Bridge)	2.1	3,880	
Yosemite Visitors Center	5.3	3,970	

YOSEMITE TO TOP OF YOSEMITE FALLS VIA YOSEMITE FALLS TRAIL AND RETURN VIA YOSEMITE POINT, NORTH DOME, AND MIRROR LAKE—20.6 MILES

Name	Distance between points	Elevation above sea level	Remarks
Yosemite Visitor Center		3,970	
Foot Yosemite Falls Trail	1.0	3,976	
Columbia Point	1.1	5,031	View Yosemite Valley
Foot Upper Yosemite Falls	0.9	5,143	View of Upper Falls
Junction Hetch Hetchy Trail	1.2	6,650	Trail branches to Hetch Hetchy, Ten Lakes, and Eagle Peak
Top Yosemite Falls	0.2	6,600	View of Yosemite Falls and Yosemite Valley
Yosemite Point	0.8	6,935	Beautiful view Yosemite Valley and High Sierra
Junction North Dome Trail	1.9	7,050	Trail branches to Tioga Road (Porcupine Flat 3.1 miles north)
North Dome	1.9	7,531	Beautiful view of Yosemite Valley. The final 700 feet to the top of the Dome is gained by means of stout steel climbing cables.
Indian Rock	1.6	8,526	Interesting rock formation
Junction Mirror Lake and Yosemite Falls Trails	1.1	8,000	Trails branch to Tioga Road (Porcupine Flat), Mirror L. and Yosemite via Yosemite Falls
Junction Tenaya Lake Trail	2.6	6,900	Trail branches to Tenaya Lake
Mirror Lake	3.9	4,082	Beautiful reflection in lake
Yosemite Visitors Center	2.4	3,970	

There is a relatively flat area of about thirteen acres on Half Dome's rounded crown which is accessible via a cable-stairway up the least precipitous approach (northeast side of Half Dome). This facility was constructed in 1919 through the cooperation of M. Hall McAllister and the Sierra Club. Yosemite Park and Curry Co. photo

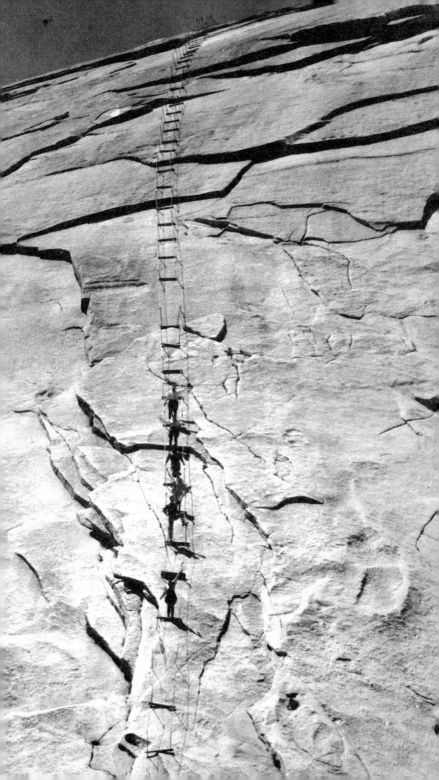

Name	Distance between points	Elevation above sea level	Remarks
Junction Hetch Hetchy and Yosemite Falls Trails		6,650	
Junction Eagle Peak Trail	0.5	6,750	
Junction Ten Lakes Trail	4.1	7,600	Trail to Ten Lakes, 10.5 miles north
Junction New Lukens Lake Trail	1.7	7,900	New Trail branches to Pate Valley
Tioga Road	0.9	8,150	
Along Tioga Road to White Wolf Meadows	3.0	8,090	Good fishing and camping
Junction White Wolf Road and Harden Lake Trail	2.0	7,600	Good camping
Junction Pate Valley Trail	0.8	7,600	Trail branches to Pate Valley, Benson Lake, and northern part of Park
Harden Lake	0.2	7,575	
Smith Meadows	5.3	6,600	Good camping; trail branches for Mather Ranger Station
Junction Hetch Hetchy Road	5.1	4,900	Road between Mather and Hetch Hetchy Dam
Along Hetch Hetchy Road to Hetch Hetchy Dam	2.4	3,826	Good fishing
Along old Lake Eleanor Road to junction Beehive Trail	3.0	5,400	Trail branches to Beehive, Laurel Lake, and Jack Main Canyon
Miguel Meadows	3.2	5,200	Good camping and grazing
Lake Eleanor Dam (junction Kibbie Ridge Trail)	3.8	4,700	Good fishing Huckleberry Lake 19 miles northeast

YOSEMITE FALLS TRAIL TO TOP OF EAGLE PEAK—6 MILES

Name	Distance between points	Elevation above sea level	Remarks
Foot Yosemite Falls Trail		3,976	
Columbia Point	1.1	5,031	
Foot of Upper Yosemite Falls	0.9	5,143	
Junction Hetch Hetchy and Yosemite Falls Trails	1.2	6,650	
Junction Eagle Peak Trail	0.5	6,750	Trail branches to Hetch Hetchy
Eagle Meadow	1.3	7,200	
Top Eagle Peak	1.0	7,773	Beautiful view of Yosemite Valley and High Sierra

MIRROR LAKE TO TUOLUMNE MEADOWS VIA TENAYA LAKE TRAIL AND THE TIOGA ROAD—21 MILES

Name	Distance between points	Elevation above sea level	Remarks
Mirror Lake		4,082	
Junction North Dome Trail	3.9	6,900	(See page 94)
Ten Mile Meadows	4.0	8,000	
Junction May Lake Trail	1.4	8,700	May Lake 3.4 miles north
Tioga Road	1.7	8,150	
Tenaya Lake	1.1	8,146	Trail branches to McGee Lake and Waterwheel Falls
Tuolumne Meadows. Ranger Station via Tioga Road	8.9	8,700	Lodge and hikers' camp accommodations

Junction Yosemite Falls and Hetch Hetchy Trails to Benson Lake via Yosemite Falls, Pate Valley, and Pleasant Valley Trails—35 Miles

Name	Distance between points	Elevation above sea level	Remarks
Junction Yosemite Falls and Hetch Hetchy Trails		6,650	
Junction Ten Lakes Trail	4.6	7,600	Trail branches to Ten Lakes
Junction New Lukens Lake Trail	1.7	7,900	Lukens Lake 2.5 miles north. Pate Valley 13.5 miles north
Tioga Road	0.9	8,150	
Along White Wolf Road to junction Harden Lake Trail	5.0	7,600	
Junction Harden Lake and Pate Valley Trails	0.8	7,600	Trail branches to Hetch Hetchy and Lake Eleanor
Pate Valley	7.7	4,500	Good camping and fishing. Trail branches to Waterwheel Falls and Tuolumne Meadows
Junction Pate Valley and Pleasant Valley Trails	4.9	8,200	Trail branches to Pleasant Valley
Rodgers Meadows (junction Rodgers Lake Trail)	4.8	9,000	Good camping and grazing. Neall Lake 0.6 mile west. Rodgers Lake 1.6 miles
Junction Benson Lake Trail	2.0	9,500	Trail branches to Tuolumne Meadows
Benson Lake	2.6	8,000	Good camping and fishing

Name	Distance between points	Elevation above sea level	Remarks
Happy Isles		4,034	
Junction Merced Lake Trail	8.2	5,950	Trail branches to Glacier Point
Little Yosemite Valley	1.2	6,150	Good camping and fishing
Junction Half Dome Trail	1.2	7,000	Top Half Dome 2.1 miles north
Junction Clouds Rest Trail	0.7	7,100	Top Clouds Rest 3.5 miles north
Junction Sunrise Trail	1.9	8,100	Merced Lake 5.7 miles east
Junction Forsyth Trail	0.1	8,150	Tenaya Lake 7.9 miles north
Long Meadow	5.2	9,500	
Cathedral Pass	3.0	9,850	Beautiful view of High Sierra
Junction Cathedral Lake Trail	1.0	9,600	Cathedral Lake 0.5 mile west
Tioga Road	3.0	8,555	Lower end Tuolumne Meadows. Good camping, fishing, and grazing
Tuolumne Ranger Station via Tioga Road	2.5	8,700	Lodge and hikers' accommodations.

HAPPY ISLES TO TUOLUMNE MEADOWS VIA VERNAL AND NEVADA FALLS, MERCED LAKE, AND BABCOCK LAKE TRAIL—29.6 MILES

Name	Distance between points	Elevation above sea level	Remarks
Happy Isles		4,034	
Little Yosemite Valley	4.4	6,150	
Junction Sunrise Trail and Forsyth Trail	3.8	8,100	
Echo Creek	3.5	6,700	Good camping, fishing, and grazing
Merced Lake	2.2	7,200	Hikers' camp accommodations
Junction Babcock Lake Trail	0.8	7,400	Washburn Lake 2.5 miles east. Lyell Fork Merced River 5 miles east
Junction Vogelsang Pass Trail	1.0	8,400	Trail branches to Vogelsang Pass and Isberg Pass
McClure Fork Merced River	0.2	8,200	Good fishing
Junction Trail to Babcock Lake	1.5	8,900	Babcock Lake 0.3 mile west
Junction Emeric Lake Trail	1.9	9,400	Emeric Lake 0.4 mile west
Boothe Lake	2.2	10,000	Good camping
Tuolumne Pass	0.8	10,200	Trail branches to Fletcher Lake. Fletcher Lake 0.8 mile south on Vogelsang Pass Trail
Junction Lyell Fork Trail	5.0	8,700	Upper end Tuolumne Meadows
Tuolumne Meadows Ranger Station	2.3	8,700	

HAPPY ISLES TO TUOLUMNE MEADOWS VIA VERNAL AND NEVADA FALLS, MERCED LAKE, AND VOGELSANG PASS TRAIL—34.2 MILES

Name	Distance between points	Elevation above sea level	Remarks
Happy Isles		4,034	
Little Yosemite Valley	4.4	6,150	
Merced Lake	9.5	7,200	Good camping and fishing
Junction Vogelsang Pass Trail	1.8	8,400	Trail branches to Babcock Lake, Boothe Lake and Tuolumne Meadows area
Junction Isberg Pass Trail	1.1	9,000	Trail branches to Isberg Pass, Post Peak Pass, and Moraine Meadows
Junction Bernice Lake Trail	2.9	9,700	Bernice Lake 1 mile east
Vogelsang Pass	1.3	10,700	Beautiful view of High Sierra
Vogelsang Lake	0.8	10,300	Good fishing
Fletcher Lake	0.9	10,150	Good fishing. Trail branches to Boothe Lake and Tuolumne Meadows via Tuolumne Pass
Evelyn Lake	1.2	10,350	
Junction Ireland Lake Trail	2.9	10,150	Ireland Lake 3 miles southwest
Junction Lyell Fork Trail	0.9	8,750	Lyell Base Camp 3 miles south. Donohue Pass 6.9 miles south
Tuolumne Meadows Ranger Station	6.5	8,700	

TUOLUMNE MEADOWS TO BOND PASS VIA WATERWHEEL FALLS, COLD CANYON, BENSON LAKE, KERRICK AND JACK MAIN CANYON TRAILS—54.7 MILES

Name	Distance between points	Elevation above sea level	Remarks
Tuolumne Meadows Ranger Station		8,700	
Junction Waterwheel Falls Trail and Tioga Road	1.2	8,594	Soda Springs
Junction Mount Conness Trail	0.8	8,700	Young Lake, 5.3 miles north; Top Mount Conness 9.2 miles north
Junction McGee Lake Trail	4.0	8,000	Tenaya Lake campsite, 6.9 miles north.
Junction Waterwheel Falls Trail	0.2	7,800	Glen Aulin (Hiker's Camp), 0.5 mi. Waterwheel Falls, 3.3 miles
Virginia Canyon (junction Virginia Pass Trail)	8.1	8,600	Virginia Pass, 5.6 miles northeast.
Matterhorn Canyon (junction Burro Pass Trail)	5.9	8,300	Burro Pass, 6.3 miles north
Benson Pass	4.4	10,139	
Smedberg Lake	2.2	9,223	Good camping
Junction Rodgers Lake Trail	1.1	9,600	Rodgers Lake 1.3 miles south; Neall L. 2.3 mi.
Junction Pleasant Valley Trail	0.6	9,500	Pleasant Valley 10 miles; Pate Valley 11.7 miles
Benson Lake	2.6	8,000	Good camping, fishing
Junction Buckeye Pass Trail (Kerrick Canyon)	3.5	8,900	Buckeye Pass 7 miles north
Junction Bear Valley Trail	3.6	8,500	Bear Valley 3 miles; Pleasant Valley 9.5 miles; Pate Valley 17.6
Stubblefield and Thompson Canyon	2.6	8,200	Good camping
Junction Tilden Lake Trail	3.2	8,300	Tilden Lake 3.1 mi. N., Tiltill Valley 9.8 mi. SW
Wilmer Lake (Jack Main Canyon)	1.8	7,800	Trail branches to Beehive, Hetch Hetchy, Yosemite Village
Junction Tilden Lake Trail	1.9	8,000	Tilden Lake, 2.3 miles
Junction Dorothy Lake Trail	6.4	9,350	Dorothy Lake, 1 mile
Bond Pass	0.6	9,750	Beautiful view High Sierra. Trail branches to Huckleberry Lake and Relief Valley Trail

Junction North Dome Trail to Bond Pass via Yosemite Falls, Pate Valley, Pleasant Valley, Bear Valley, and Jack Main Canyon—54.8 Miles

Name	Distance between points	Elevation above sea level	Remarks
Junction North Dome Trail		6,650	(See page 94)
Junction Ten Lakes Trail	4.6	7,600	
Tioga Road	2.6	8,150	
Along Tioga Road to junction Pate Valley Trail	5.0	7,600	Trail branches to Hetch Hetchy and Pate Valley
Junction Harden Lake Trail	0.8	7,600	Trail branches to Hetch Hetchy
Pate Valley	7.7	4,500	Trail branches to Waterwheel Falls and Tuolumne Meadows
Junction Pleasant Valley Trail	4.9	8,200	Trail branches to Benson Lake and Rodgers Lake
Pleasant Valley	3.2	6,900	Good camping, fishing, and grazing
Junction Bear Valley and Rancheria Trails	2.0	8,150	Trail branches to Rancheria Mountain and Tiltill Valley. Tiltill Valley, 12 miles west
Bear Valley	4.5	9,500	Good camping and grazing
Junction Kerrick Canyon Trail	3.0	8,500	Trail branches to Benson Lake, Buckeye Pass, and Tuolumne Meadows
Stubblefield and Thompson Canyons	2.6	8,200	Good camping and grazing
Wilmer Lake (Jack Main Canyon)	5.0	7,800	Beehive, 11.2 miles southwest; Hetch Hetchy, 17.5 miles southwest; Yosemite, 47.7 miles southwest
Junction Alden Lake Trail	1.9	8,000	Tilden Lake, 2.3 miles northeast
Bond Pass	7.0	9,350	Beautiful view of High Sierra. Trail branches for Huckleberry Lake and Relief Valley Trail

Name	Distance between points	Elevation above sea level	Remarks
Junction North Dome Trail		6,650	(See page 84)
Tioga Road	7.2	8,150	
Along Tioga Road to junction Harden Lake Trail	5.0	7,600	
Junction Pate Valley Trail	0.8	7,600	Pate Valley, 7.7 miles east
Smith Meadows to junction Mather Trail	5.5	6,000	Trail branches to summit of Smith Peak and Mather Ranger Station. Mather Ranger Station, 6.6 miles southwest. Summit Smith Peak, 1 mile north
Junction Hetch Hetchy Road	5.1	4,900	Road between Mather and Hetch Hetchy Dam
Along Hetch Hetchy Road to Hetch Hetchy Dam	2.4	3,826	Good fishing
Along Old Eleanor Road to Junction Beehive Trail	3.0	5,400	Lake Eleanor 7 miles west
Beehive (junction Laurel Lake Trail)	3.3	6,500	Laurel Lake 1.2 miles west. Good fishing
Junction Lake Vernon Trail			Trail branches to Jack Main Canyon; Wilmer Lake 9.9 miles; Bond Pass 18.8 miles
Lake Vernon	2.3	6,000	Good fishing
Tiltill Valley	6.0	5,675	Trail branches to Pleasant Valley 14 miles east. Jack Main Canyon 10 miles north

NORTH DOME TRAIL JUNCTION TO TUOLUMNE MEADOWS VIA
YOSEMITE FALLS, PATE VALLEY, AND WATERWHEEL
FALLS TRAILS—41.3 MILES

Name	Distance between points	Elevation above sea level	Remarks
Junction North Dome Trail		6,650	
Tioga Road	7.2	8,150	
Along Tioga Road to Junction Pate Valley Trail	5.0	7,600	Good camping and fishing
Junction Harden Lake Trail	0.8	7,600	Trail branches to Mather and Hetch Hetchy
Pate Valley	7.7	4,500	Trail branches to Pleasant Valley, Benson Lake, and Rodgers Lake
Muir Gorge	4.1	5,000	River flows through narrow gorge
Waterwheel Falls	7.0	6,500	Beautiful waterfalls
Le Conte Falls	0.6	7,000	Same as above
California Falls	0.7	7,500	Same as above
Glen Aulin	1.5	7,800	Hikers' camp accommodations
Junction Cold Canyon Trail	0.5	7,900	Trail branches to Virginia Canyon, Benson Lake, and Jack Main Canyon
Junction McGee Lake Trail	0.2	8,000	Tenaya Lake 6.9 miles south (campsite). Yosemite 21.4 miles south
Tioga Road (Tuolumne Meadows, Soda Springs)	4.8	8,594	Good camping and fishing
Along Tioga Road to Tuolumne Meadows Ranger Station	1.2	8,700	

Yosemite to Moraine Meadows via Glacier Point and Merced Pass and Return via Fernandez Pass, Post Peak Pass, Merced Lake, and Nevada and Vernal Falls—65.1 Miles

Name	Distance between points	Elevation above sea level	Remarks
Yosemite Visitor Center		3,970	
Glacier Point via Short Trail	4.9	7,214	
Junction Buena Vista and Nevada Falls Trails	1.5	6,400	Trail branches to Yosemite via Nevada and Vernal Falls
Junction Mono Meadows Trail	2.2	6,500	Mono Meadows 2.3 miles west
Junction Buena Vista and Merced Pass Trails	0.1	6,500	Trail branches to Johnson Lake and Buck Camp
Junction of trail to Yosemite via Nevada Falls	0.1	6,500	Yosemite via Nevada Falls, 9.6 miles
Second junction of trail to Yosemite via Nevada Falls	1.7	7,000	Yosemite via Nevada Falls, 10.1 miles
Merced Pass	8.6	9,295	
Junction Moraine Meadows Trail	1.9	8,800	Trail branches to Buck Camp, Johnson Lake, and Wawona
Moraine Meadows (junction Chain Lakes Trail)	1.2	8,700	Chain Lakes 2.7 miles south. Chiquito Pass 5.9 miles south
Junction Breeze Lake Trail	2.7	9,500	Breeze Lake 0.5 mile south
Fernandez Pass	0.7	10,175	Beautiful view of High Sierra
Junction Post Peak Trail	1.6	9,000	Trail branches to Clover Meadows and Devils Post Pile
Post Peak Pass	6.1	10,800	Beautiful view of High Sierra
Junction Isberg Pass Trail	0.5	10,300	Trail branches to Isberg Pass, Sadler Lake, Little Jackass Meadows
Lyell Fork Merced River	6.5	9,100	Good camping and fishing
Junction Vogelsang Pass Trail	5.6	9,000	Trail branches to Vogelsang Pass and Tuolumne Meadows

(Continued)

Name	Distance between points	Elevation above sea level	Remarks
(Continued from facing page)			
Junction Babcock Lake Trail	1.1	8,400	Trail branches to Babcock and Boothe Lakes and Tuolumne Meadows
Junction Washburn Lake Trail	1.0	7,400	Trail branches to Washburn Lake
Merced Lake	0.8	7,200	Hikers' camp accommodations
Yosemite via Nevada and Vernal Falls	16.3	3,970	(See page 37)

GLACIER POINT TO MORAINE MEADOWS VIA BUENA VISTA TRAIL—23.4 MILES

Name	Distance between points	Elevation above sea level	Remarks
Glacier Point		7,214	
Junction Buena Vista and Merced Lake Trails	3.8	6,500	Trail branches to Merced Pass and Yosemite via Nevada Falls
Buena Vista Lake	9.3	9,300	Good fishing
Buena Vista Pass	0.6	9,600	Beautiful view
Royal Arch Lake	2.0	8,850	Good camping and fishing
Junction Buck Camp Trail	0.8	8,600	Johnson Lake 0.8 mile west; Wawona 13.1 miles west
Buck Camp	1.3	8,250	Good camping
Junction Chiquito Lake Trail	1.1	8,400	Chiquito Pass 3.6 miles south; Soda Springs 3.5 miles south. South Fork Merced River; good fishing. Chain Lakes 4.8 miles south
Junction Givens Lake Trail	1.7	8,800	Givens Lake 1 mile west. Good fishing
Junction Merced Pass Trail	1.4	8,800	Trail branches to Yosemite via Merced Pass
Moraine Meadows (junction Chain Lakes Trail)	1.2	8,700	Chain Lakes 2.7 miles south; Chiquito Pass 5.9 miles south

Name	Distance between points	Elevation above sea level	Remarks
Glacier Point		7,214	
Junction Sentinel Dome Trail	0.6	7,600	Sentinel Dome 0.5 mile west
Along Glacier Point Road	—	—	Road between Chinquapin and Glacier Point
Junction Pohono Trail and Glacier Point Road	1.0	7,725	Trail branches to Yosemite via Taft Point and Inspiration Point on Wawona Road
Junction Buck Camp Trail and Glacier Point Road	4.2	7,100	Good camping and grazing
Junction Ostrander Lake Trail	2.5	7,200	Ostrander Lake 5 miles east
Junction trail to Chinquapin	2.5	7,800	Alder Creek Trail 3.3 miles west; Chinquapin 9.5 miles west (Wawona Road)
Junction trail to Wawona via Chilnualna Falls	1.4	7,600	Wawona 8.3 miles southwest
Second junction trail to Wawona via Chilnualna Falls	1.6	7,800	Wawona 8.1 miles southwest
Grouse Lake	2.0	8,300	Good fishing
Crescent Lake	1.1	8,521	Good camping and fair fishing
Johnson Lake	1.1	8,500	Good camping and fishing
Junction Buena Vista Trail	0.8	8,600	Trail branches to Yosemite via Buena Vista Pass and Glacier Point
Buck Camp	1.3	8,250	Good camping

GLACIER POINT TO WAWONA VIA POHONO AND ALDER CREEK TRAILS—21.3 MILES

Name	Distance between points	Elevation above sea level	Remarks
Glacier Point		7,214	
Junction Pohono Trail and Glacier Point Road	1.6	7,725	
Taft Point and The Fissures	1.1	7,503	Beautiful view of Yosemite Valley. Fissures are several hundred feet deep
Bridalveil Creek	2.1	6,700	Good fishing
Junction Alder Creek Trail	0.2	7,000	Inspiration Point 8.2 miles west (Wawona Road). Yosemite 13.5 miles
McGirk Meadows	1.2	7,000	
Glacier Point Road	1.3	7,150	
Old Railroad Grade	2.7	7,100	From this point trail follows along old railroad grade
Junction Buck Camp Trail	0.8	7,050	Trail branches to Buck Camp Trail 3.3 miles east. Buck Camp 12.6 miles east
Junction Chinquapin Trail (Empire Meadows)	1.2	7,000	Chinquapin 5 miles northwest
Alder Creek	2.2	5,900	
End old Railroad Grade	1.5	6,000	Trail leaves grade and follows old Alder Creek Trail
Mosquito Camp Trail	2.1	5,500	
Wawona Road (South Fork Merced River)	3.1	4,050	Chilnualna Falls Trail branches
Wawona	0.2	4,096	Hotel and camp accommodations

Wawona to Johnson Lake via Chilnualna Falls Trail—12.3 Miles

Name	Distance between points	Elevation above sea level	Remarks
Wawona		4,096	
Junction Chilnualna Road and Wawona Road	0.2	4,050	Chilnualna Road is a service road
Along Chilnualna Road to Junction Chilnualna Falls Trail	1.3	4,300	Chilnualna Falls Trail
Top Chilnualna Falls	3.7	6,500	Beautiful falls and cascades
Junction trail to Yosemite via Buck Camp Trail	0.3	6,700	Buck Camp Trail 2.8 miles north; Yosemite 19.9 miles north
Chilnualna Creek (Chilnualna Ranger Station)	0.6	6,900	Good camping and fishing
Junction Buck Camp Trail	2.0	7,800	Yosemite via Glacier Point 18.7 miles; Chinquapin 12.5 miles (Wawona Road)
Grouse Lake	2.0	8,300	Good fishing
Crescent Lake	1.1	8,521	Good camping and fair fishing
Johnson Lake	1.1	8,500	Good camping and fishing

Mirror Lake to Waterwheel Falls via Tenaya Lake and McGee Lake and Return via Pate Valley, Harden Lake, and Yosemite Falls—58.5 Miles

Name	Distance between points	Elevation above sea level	Remarks
Mirror Lake		4,082	
Tenaya Lake (junction McGee Lake Trail)	12.1	8,146	Good camping and fishing
McGee Lake	6.3	8,100	
Junction Waterwheel Falls Trail	0.6	8,000	Tuolumne Meadows Ranger Station 6 miles east

(*Continued*)

Name	Distance between points	Elevation above sea level	Remarks
(*Continued from facing page*)			
Junction Cold Canyon Trail	0.2	7,900	
Glen Aulin	0.5	7,800	
Waterwheel Falls	2.8	6,500	
Muir Gorge	7.0	5,000	
Pate Valley (junction Pleasant Valley Trail)	4.1	4,500	(See page 93)
Hardin Lake (junction Hardin Lake Trail)	7.7	7,600	
Tioga Road	0.8	7,600	
Junction Tioga Road and Yosemite Trail	5.0	8,150	
Yosemite	11.4	3,970	

YOSEMITE FALLS TRAIL TO TEN LAKES VIA YOSEMITE FALLS AND YOSEMITE CREEK RANGER STATION—15.1 MILES

Name	Distance between points	Elevation above sea level	Remarks
Junction Yosemite Falls Trail		6,650	(See page 96)
Junction Hetch Hetchy Trail	4.6	7,600	
Tioga Road (Yosemite Creek)	1.8	7,200	Good camping
Along Tioga Road to junction Ten Lakes Trail	0.4	7,200	
Junction White Wolf Trail	4.1	8,300	Tioga Road (White Wolf Meadows) 5.7 miles west. Good camping
Half Moon Meadow	1.8	9,100	
Junction Grant Lakes Trail	0.9	9,600	Grant Lakes 1.1 miles southeast
Ten Lakes Pass	0.2	9,750	Beautiful view
Ten Lakes	1.3	9,200	Good camping and fishing

THE HIGH SIERRA LOOP TRAILS

Of the 1,189 square miles within the boundaries of Yosemite National Park, more than 1,100 lie in the vast High Sierra region west of the crest of the Sierra Nevada Range. This is a fabulous stretch of mountains, defying adequate description but possessed of jagged peaks—tumbling streams—friendly meadows dotted with delicate blossoms—deep blue lakes lying in the shadows of glacier-scarred cliffs—and green forests which change in nature as the elevation rises from the cedars, pines, and firs of the lower levels to the wind-twisted hemlocks and white bark pine of the higher altitudes.

Arranged roughly in a circle are six permanent summer High Sierra Camps. On the average, these are located about nine miles apart and each of the six is at an area of outstanding beauty and interest. Camps provide accommodations in tents housing beds with springs and mattresses, linen and ample blankets. Breakfast and dinner are served in a central dining tent and, though simple, the quality and preparation are excellent and quantities ample. There are hot showers at each camp, which are a welcome luxury in the wilderness, especially at the end of a day on the trail. Other essential plumbing is enclosed and of the running-water type. Early September sees the closing of the High Sierra camps.

May Lake Camp. (Elevation 9,270 feet. 9.8 miles from Yosemite Valley; 8.6 miles to Glen Aulin Camp; 8 miles to Sunrise Camp.) The trail to May Lake Camp leaves Yosemite Valley at Mirror Lake (see page 45) and climbs up and out of Tenaya Canyon by way of the "Tenaya Zigzags." The trail crosses the Tioga Road near Snow Flat, so called because of the heavy snowpack which piles up there during the winter months. A mile beyond, at the foot of towering Mount Hoffmann, lies May Lake, and on its eastern shore in a beautiful setting of mountain hemlocks is the camp itself. Just beneath the northern wall of Mount Hoffmann (10,921 feet) is the horseshoe-shaped head of Yosemite Creek, with its numerous little glacier-scooped lakelets; this head, with its deep snow banks, forms the main source of Yosemite Creek. Miles below, Yosemite Creek leaps over the wall of the Valley at an elevation of 6,525 feet to become Yosemite Falls. A promontory behind the camp affords one of the most spectacular panoramas in the whole Sierra—a full sweep of Tenaya Canyon from Half Dome at its foot to Tenaya Lake at its head, with Cathedral Peak boldly outlined against the horizon. On clear evenings you can see the Firefall at Glacier Point from here.

Mount Hoffmann and Tenaya Peak are splendid side trips for those with some climbing experience. During years of normal winter snows in the Sierra the north slope of Mount Hoffmann offers good skiing even up to July. From its summit one will see a superb view of the Park, for Mount Hoffmann is at the center, and well above nearby peaks. In mid-summer, over 100 varieties of wildflowers can be counted on Mount Hoffmann and neighboring slopes. Naturalist John Muir said of it, "On no other Yosemite Park Mountain are you more likely to linger." Tenaya Peak, which overlooks Tenaya Lake, rises to an elevation of 10,300 feet.

Glen Aulin Camp. (Elevation 7,800 feet. 8.6 miles from May Lake; 7.6 miles to Tuolumne Meadows Lodge.) Following the McGee Lake Trail (see page 100), across high ridges, you drop down into Glen Aulin. The camp is at the foot of the White Cascade on the Tuolumne River. You will probably notice many vertical scratches in the smooth white bark of the aspens below camp. These are bear clawmarks, and the Park naturalists feel that the bear making the highest scratches is claiming "title" to that area. Perhaps the most phenomenal of Glen Aulin scenes is the series of falls made by the river in its spectacular drop to the Grand Canyon of the Tuolumne. California, Le Conte, and the famous Waterwheel Falls are literally "upside down" falls, where ridges and depressions in the river bed toss the turbulent stream in magnificent arcs of white water 30 to 40 feet high, during the early season. To be certain that you see the finest of these waterwheels, follow the river to Return Creek junction.

One of the most interesting side trips in this area is Muir Gorge. This gorge (9.9 miles) is a narrow, deep box canyon through which the Tuolumne River flows. The trail climbs several hundred feet above the river at this point, and continues to Pate Valley and Harden Lake, near the Tioga Road (see page 101). The Tuolumne Canyon provides a trip well worthwhile for those who do not wish to fish. The falls and cascades that dash down the canyon sides are most striking.

Tuolumne Meadows Lodge. (Elevation 8,600 feet. 7.6 miles from Glen Aulin Camp; 7.2 miles to Vogelsang Camp via Rafferty Creek; 12.3 miles to Vogelsang Camp via Ireland Creek; 11 miles to Sunrise Camp.) The trail from Glen Aulin to Tuolumne Mead-

ows takes you along the Tuolumne River, past White Cascade and Tuolumne Falls, then on to Soda Springs, where you can drink real soda water, and across the Tioga Road to Tuolumne Meadows Lodge. The Lodge, located on the Dana Fork just below Dana Cascade, is the largest of the six High Sierra Camps.

If you climb no other peak during your High Sierra trip you should see the tremendous extent of the Sierran Crest, the desert ranges receding into the eastern haze, the western foothills and perhaps the Coast Range, the blue expanse of Mono Lake 6,627 feet beneath, from the summit of Mount Dana. It is a long but easy climb (3 miles—3,100 feet) from Tioga Pass. Mount Dana, elevation 13,053 feet, is the third highest peak in the Park. From Tioga Pass the Dana Glacier is 3 miles off-trail along the stream flowing into Tioga Lake. Below the glacier are several newly formed moraines and lakes of the milky-blue hue peculiar to water containing glacial silt.

Horses may be taken to 10,500 feet on the Lyell Fork Trail, where it turns east to cross Donohue Pass. The route to the Lyell glaciers is well marked with ducks (1 or 2 rocks atop another). Be sure to apply your favorite sunburn preventive generously and wear dark glasses before venturing upon the ice for any distance. Mount Lyell, elevation 13,114 feet, highest in the Park, and Mount Maclure, may be climbed from the head of the westerly glacier. The trip usually requires two days and considerable climbing experience.

Sunrise Camp. (Elevation 9,400 feet. 11 miles from Tuolumne Meadows; 10 miles from Merced Camp; 8 miles from May Lake Camp.) The Sunrise Trail from Tuolumne Meadows leaves the Tioga Road at Budd Creek, about 3 miles west of the Tuolumne Meadows Lodge. The first mile of the trail is quite steep as it twists through forests mainly of lodgepole pines. At about 3 miles, the trail to Lower Cathedral Lake is intersected; the lake lies about 0.5 of a mile west.

There are many marvelous mountain views along the Sunrise Trail near and at the summit of Cathedral Pass. From the pass, the trail descends gently toward Long Meadows, passing Columbia

---

Hiking the Tuolumne trails into high country is an outstanding experience. Above hikers are seen in the Mount Maclure region.
Yosemite Park and Curry Co. photo

Finger to the right. The trail follows the meadow's edge with the Sunrise Camp near its end. Located on a boulder-strewn bench about 30-40 feet above the meadow, Sunrise presents an inconspicuous appearance to a hiker or rider on the trail so carefully have the tents been dispersed.

Within 5 miles of Sunrise Camp there are several peaks that present interesting and challenging climbs. Columbia Finger, Tresidder Peak, Echo Peaks are difficult scrambles and should not be undertaken by inexperienced climbers. An easier hike and one quite enjoyable is the 10 mile (round trip) hike to Clouds Rest. Take the trail from camp to the Forsythe Trail junction, then turn left (south) and follow it about 1½ miles to the Clouds Rest Trail junction. It is now about a mile to the summit. One may return by the above route or continue south on the Forsythe Trail to its intersection with the Sunrise Trail. Here, turn to the left (north) and return to camp over Sunrise Mountain. NOTE: The trail to Merced Lake intersects the Sunrise Trail at about the same point where it intersects the Forsythe Trail. So be sure you are headed back (north) to Sunrise Camp, not to Merced Lake.

Vogelsang Camp. (Elevation 10,300 feet. 7.2 miles from Tuolumne Meadows Lodge via Rafferty Creek; 12.3 miles via Ireland Creek; 9.1 miles to Merced Lake Camp via Vogelsang Pass; 7.6 miles via Babcock Lake.) The Vogelsang area was a great gathering ground for glaciers during the Ice Age. Numerous glacial cirques abound, offering striking evidence as to the birthplace of a glacier. The frail, knife-edged peaks, such as Vogelsang, were always above the highest limits reached by glacial ice. Another bit of glacial evidence is the step formation of the canyons, some steps containing a lake or two in the hollows excavated by the ice. There are nine steps on the Lewis Creek, others at Merced Lake, Lost Valley, Little Yosemite, and finally Yosemite Valley—the grandest of all.

From Vogelsang Pass (10,700 feet), experienced mountaineers may climb Vogelsang Peak, to a view as fine as may be found in the Park. Parsons Peak cirque is southeast of camp at the Headwaters of Fletcher Creek. Here you will find four lakes above Fletcher Lake, the highest at 10,500 feet, above which the precipitous glacier-cut walls of the cirque rise nearly 2,000 feet to Parsons Peak. Rafferty Peak is climbed from Tuolumne Pass. Precipices drop abruptly from the summit into Echo Creek basin, across which you will see some of the most difficult Yosemite peaks—Cathedral, Echo, and the Cockscomb.

106

Merced Lake Camp. (Elevation 7,150 feet. 9.1 miles from Vogel-sang Camp via Vogelsang Pass; 7.6 miles from Vogelsang Camp via Babcock Lake; 12.4 miles to Happy Isles, Yosemite Valley; 10 miles from Sunrise Camp.) The trail between Merced Lake and Yosemite Valley is one of the most spectacular in the Park. Skirting the lake, it passes through a beautiful grove of aspen, through forests of pine and fir, then suddenly emerges onto a broad expanse of glacier-polished granite. Soon the acres of granite disappear and the trail enters Lost Valley, then winds through Little Yosemite Valley on past Nevada and Vernal Falls, and down the steep walls of the Merced Canyon to Happy Isles on the floor of Yosemite Valley.

For those with climbing and off-trail experience there are many interesting side trips in the Merced Lake area. Mount Clark (6 miles), Gray Peak (7.5 miles), and Adair Lake, elevation 10,300 feet (7 miles) with its goldent trout, are accessible from Gray Peak Fork. From the Isberg Pass trail one may penetrate an immense glacial amphitheater at the head of the Lyell Fork (11 miles) where 23 lakelets (no trout) are surrounded by splendid peaks—Lyell, Maclure, Rodgers, Electra, Foerster and two without names that are apparently unclimbed.

A High Sierra trip was once thought to be only for those of extraordinary strength and endurance. The presence of the comfortable camps located at convenient distances apart make either a hiking or riding trip quite possible for "early-middle age" people, and along the trail and at the campfire one finds more than a few grandparents. There are several organized trips along these trails.

Six-day Saddle Trip. Three times weekly during the summer season, the Yosemite Park and Curry Co. operates fine six-day saddle trips originating and ending in Yosemite Valley. These trips are limited to ten persons, and an experienced guide accompanies each group. As there are two routes between Tuolumne Meadows Lodge and Merced Lake Camp, one via Vogelsang Camp, the other via the newest, Sunrise Camp, trips follow one of these on alternating schedules. Mules provide transportation on this trip, having been found trailwise, sure-footed and somewhat more comfortable to sit astride than horses. Personal necessities (see page 76) are limited to 10 pounds per person and are carried on a pack mule. The saddle trip is arranged on an all-expense basis and the rate includes all meals, dormitory tent accommodations, saddle animal, and guide service.

107

Four-day Saddle Trip. For those with too little time to take the six-day trip, a four-day group trip departs weekly from Tuolumne Meadows, stopping a night at Glen Aulin, May Lake, Sunrise Camp, returning to the Meadows on the fourth day.

Seven-day Hiking Trip. For those who wish to hike the Yosemite "loop" trail, seven-day hiking trips make the circle of camps each week. Fifteen is the maximum on each trip and a Park Naturalist is in charge. He points out and explains features of the trailside—the flowers, trees, birds, geology—so that hiking-party members come to know intimately the natural things encountered. The trip begins from Tuolumne Meadows Lodge. Because hiking at elevations of 7,000 to 10,000 feet is more demanding than at lower elevations, it is advised that hiking-party members spend about a day at Tuolumne Meadows to become somewhat accustomed to the more rarefied air. From Tuolumne the hiking party spends one night each in the following order: at Glen Aulin Camp, May Lake Camp, Sunrise Camp, two nights at Merced Lake Camp, one night at Vogelsang Camp, returning to Tuolumne Meadows on the seventh day.

THE JOHN MUIR TRAIL

The John Muir Trail traces the backbone of the Sierra Nevada Range between Yosemite Valley on the north and Whitney Portal on the south—a distance of 218 miles. Over this entire route the trail makes contact with roads in four places: Yosemite Valley, Tuolumne Meadows, Devils Postpile National Monument, and Whitney Portal. (Mount Whitney, with an elevation of 14,495 feet is second only to Mount McKinley as the highest peak in the United States.) Thirty-six miles of the trail lies in the Sierra, Inyo, and Mono National Forests and Sequoia and Kings Canyon National Parks.

The best time to travel the trail is between July 15 and September 15, depending upon snow conditions. It should be remembered that most of the trail is at elevations of more than 7,000 feet, and in some places goes above 13,000 feet.

Perhaps the best source of information on the John Muir Trail is *Starr's Guide to the John Muir Trail and the High Sierra Region* (map of the trail included). This publication may be secured from the Yosemite Natural History Association. A topographic map covering the section of the John Muir Trail within Yosemite National Park may also be obtained from the Yosemite Natural History Association (see page 202). Maps of other sections of the trail may be secured from the U.S. Forest Service Regional Office, San Francisco, California. Maps of Sequoia and Kings Canyon National Park, Three Rivers, California 93271.

BACK-COUNTRY ETIQUETTE
AND REGULATIONS

A party desiring to make either a pack or hiking trip into the back country, on their own without benefit of a guide, must do the following:

1. Go to a ranger station and obtain a campfire permit for the area or areas they will be in. Even with a permit, a fire can only be built at an approved back-country campfire site. A list of these locations may be obtained from the District Ranger who issues the fire permit.

2. Give their itinerary to the Ranger. This is necessary for several reasons, including protection of the visitor and the protection of the Park. Never hike alone.

3. Always report the completion of your trip to prevent a needless search, and turn in the campfire permit at the same time.

In addition, keep the following back-country etiquette and regulations in mind:

1. The use or even carrying of guns is prohibited.

2. Dogs or cats are not permitted in any of the back country of the Park—not even on leash.

3. Motorcycles, or other motor vehicles, or bicycles, boats, or portable motors such as power plants and chain saws, are not permitted in the back country.

4. Destruction, injury, defacement, or removal or disturbance in any manner of public property or any natural features or object is prohibited. This includes: (a) the shooting or molesting of any bird or wild animals, or the picking of flowers or other plants; (b) the cutting, blazing, marking, driving nails in, or otherwise damaging of growing trees or standing snags—no pine boughs or ferns for beds; (c) the writing, carving, or painting of name or other inscription anywhere; and (d) the destruction, defacement, or moving of signs.

5. Collecting specimens of plants, minerals, animal life, or other natural or historical objects is prohibited without written authorization, obtained in advance, from the Superintendent. Permits are not issued for personal collections.

6. Conserve wood by keeping fires as small as possible. Firewood is scarce in many areas above 9,500 feet elevation. If you are traveling with stock it would be wise to bring a gasoline stove.

7. Build your fires where other have had fires in already established fire-places. This conserves clean camping space and does not make new scars.

8. Do not litter the trail. While traveling, put your gum, candy, and cigarette wrappers in your pocket to start your next campfire.

9. Where there are no toilet facilities, go well away from campsites, trails, lakes, or streams. Dig your latrine and cover it when leaving.

10. You are required to clean your camp before you leave. Burn your garbage. Leaving food and garbage encourages bears and other animals to raid campsites. Do not bury it, or cans, as animals will dig it up, leaving an unsightly mess. Thus, tin cans, foil, glass, worn-out or useless gear, and other unburnables must be carried out of the back country with you.

11. Keep the waters clean. Your activities must be governed to prevent the pollution of lakes and streams. Do not use soap directly in the water source, and don't throw wash water, fish entrails, garbage, or trash in the water.

12. Pack outfits and saddle horses have the right-of-way on trails. Hikers should get completely off the trail on the low side and remain quiet until the stock has passed.

13. Loose herding of pack and saddle animals on park trails is prohibited, except certain designated hazardous trails. If you are bringing your own stock into the Parks, write for a copy of the grazing and loose herding regulations.

14. Taking short cuts on switchbacks is prohibited. Keeping to the trails is safer, easier and prevents harmful erosion.

15. With the increase in back-country travel, it is more important than ever before that everyone adheres to the rules of common courtesy and good mountain manners. A wilderness outing can offer many things; but to most people it is the solitude, peace, and quiet that is most important. Yelling and unnecessary noise are out of place in the wilderness. Do not crowd the other fellow by camping beside him. Chances are if he wanted company he'd have camped in a front-country automobile camp-ground.

Chapter 5.

Plantlife of the Park

Few places in the United States have a wider variety of native plants and animals than the Sierran slopes. Within Yosemite National Park, from the warm foothills near Arch Rock at 2,000 feet above sea level to the windy summits of peaks like 13,114-foot-high Mount Lyell, there are five easy-to-recognize assemblages of plants and animals. These are roughly arranged in belts. As you ascend the slopes, you go from one such belt to another. At first the change is hardly noticeable; then, the altered scenery makes you realize you are surrounded by a different community of plant (flora) and animal (fauna) life.

While several concepts have been proposed for describing plant-animal distributional assemblages—including the biotic provinces, plant belts, plant-animal communities, and Dr. C. Hart Merriam's life zones—no one system is perfect for any great area of the United States because the subject is very complex and the controlling factors are not completely understood. For many years the "life zone" theory was employed by the naturalists of Yosemite National Park to explain plant and animal distribution. Recently, it was found that the "plant belt" concept best describes the distributional assemblages in the Park.

PLANT BELTS OF THE PARK

Though an accepted theory for quite a few years, the basic importance of the plant-belt idea is witnessed by definition. A plant belt is a zone or area having uniform constitution with respect to flora and fauna. The boundary between two plant belts is seldom

GRIZZLY GIANT

clear-cut or straight; rather the belts are slightly entwined. While some species of plants and animals are restricted to a single belt, the majority occupy two or three belts although not always in equal numbers, and a few are present in any belt where their particular ecologic (habitat) requirements are fulfilled. Roughly, the altitudinal boundaries of both the plant belt and life zones concepts in Yosemite National Park are as follows:

Belt	Life Zone	Altitudinal Boundaries
Foothill or Digger Pine-Chaparral	Upper Sonoran	800 to 4,000 feet
Yellow Pine	Transition	2,000 to 6,500 feet
Lodgepole pine-Red Fir	Canadian	6,500 to 8,000 feet
Subalpine	Hudsonian	7,500 to 10,500 feet
Alpine	Arctic-Alpine	10,500 feet and up

Some place names closely identified with the various belts in the Yosemite region are:

Foothill Belt	Pleasant Valley, El Portal, Arch Rock Entrance
Yellow Pine Belt	Yosemite Valley, Crane Flat, Big Oak Flat Road, Wawona Road
Lodgepole Pine-Red Fir Belt	Glacier Point, Merced Lake, White Wolf
Subalpine Belt	Tioga Pass, Tenaya Lake, Tuolumne Meadows
Alpine Belt	Mount Dana and Mount Lyell

CONE-BEARING TREES OF THE PARK

The forests of Yosemite National Park are primarily conifer (cone-bearing trees). Their leaves are retained from two to ten years, which often causes them to be called evergreens.

The Grizzly Giant in the Mariposa Grove is considered the oldest tree in the Park; its age is estimated at over 27,000 years. National Park Service photo

113

The pines (*Pinus*) are represented in the Park by nine species, some of which may be found at almost any altitude. The characteristic distinguishing this from all other genera is the occurrence of the needles in bundles of 5, 4, 3, or 2 (and in one species singly), the base of each bundle being surrounded by a paperlike sheath. The 5-needle pines are called the "white pines" and those with 3 needles the "yellow pines."

Of the three 5-needle pines of the Park, the Sugar Pine (*Pinus Lambertiana*) is by far the most important. It is not only the largest pine in the world but also one of the most majestically beautiful. It may easily be recognized by its carmine-brown flaky bark which is generally divided into long plates by longitudinal fissures; by its 5-needle bundles about 3 inches in length; and by the immense cones (12 to 24 inches long) which hang pendent from the tips of the long straight horizontal branches, or which may be found on the forest floor beneath. A white sugar which exudes from the heartwood when the tree is wounded gives it its common name. On the floor of the Valley are but few specimens, but a short distance up the slopes (along the Wawona and Big Oak Flat Roads) the species enters into the forest composition and grows abundantly up to about 7,500 feet elevation.

The Western White Pine (*Pinus monticola*) which forms an important part of the forests of Idaho and Montana, occurs in California—the southern part of its range—only on the higher mountain slopes, ranging in the Park from 8,000 feet to timberline. It occurs along the Glacier Point Road, and several small trees grow out of cracks in the bare granite of Sentinel Dome. Trees are numerous along the upper parts of the trails to Half Dome and Clouds Rest, and are easily observed along the Tioga Road from White Wolf to Tioga Pass. The young trees with their bluish-green foliage and silvery-gray bark are exceedingly symmetrical. Trees over 2 feet in diameter take on a more rugged appearance, and their bark, which then continuously flakes off, checks into very distinctive 5-sided grayish-purple plates. The tree is one of the largest in the sub-alpine forests and may be distinguished by its 5-needle bundles which range from 2 to 4 inches in length; by its long feathery cones (length 5 to 8 inches) which are borne in clusters at the ends of the long straight branches; and by the very characteristic 5-sided small plates in the bark of the older trees.

Hardiest of all Yosemite trees is the 5-needled Whitebark Pine (*Pinus albicaulis*). A few large specimens 2½ feet in diameter

114

and up to 30 feet in height are sometimes encountered between 9,000 and 10,000 feet elevation, but the species is most evident at timberline where it forms a scattered forest of dwarf or prostrate trees. These trees, always in keeping with their bleak surroundings, are the delight of the mountaineer. (The most accessible place to see Whitebark Pine in Yosemite National Park is Tioga Pass.) Specimens may be identified by having 5 short leaves per bundle (length 1½ to 2½ inches) which are tufted at the ends of the flexible branchlets; by the small hard cones (about the size of a hen's egg); and by the smooth white bark.

In the deep Merced Canyon, Digger Pine (*Pinus Sabiniana*) grows sparsely from the western Park boundary to an elevation of 2,000 feet near Arch Rock. Near Wawona, a few trees occur at the 5,000-foot elevation. In the Hetch Hetchy region, the habitat is more suitable for this species, and the trees are rather abundant. The Digger Pine's wide-branching habit and spare silvery-gray foliage set it apart from all other species. Most important of its distinguishing characteristics are the gray-green clusters of long flexible leaves (length 8½ to 12 inches) which occur 3 in a bundle; the low-branching habit; and the large heavily armed cones which generally remain on the trees.

Least important of the Park's four yellow pines is the Knob-Cone Pine (*Pinus attenuata*). It is rare in the forests of Yosemite National Park, but ranges in elevation from 3,000 to 6,000 feet. It has a broad crown and its trunk is forked near the middle; it is then like the Digger Pine, but smaller. The tree might be mistaken for the Digger Pine, but can usually be distinguished by its many clusters of small cones. The needles of Knob-Cone Pine are pale yellow-green, and 3 to 5 inches long (quite short for a 3-needled pine). They droop like those of Digger Pine, but are more evenly distributed along the branches, rather than being tasseled at the branch tips.

The Ponderosa Pine (*Pinus ponderosa*) and Jeffrey Pine (*Pinus Jeffreyi*) have many similar characteristics. Both trees reach a large size (maximum diameter 8 to 10 feet) and are tall and symmetrical. They are exceedingly abundant within the Park. The rich green foliage is made up of 3-needle bundles which range from 5 to 11 inches in length. The flaky bark of all older trees is distinctively divided into large yellow plates by deep fissures. The Ponderosa Pine ranges at elevations from 3,000 to 6,500 feet, while the Jeffrey Pine is found from 5,750 to 8,750 feet. (Scattered trees of each species occur both above and below these ranges.)

The chief contrasts between the two species are in the cones, which are 2½ to 5½ inches in length in the Ponderosa Pine and 5½ to 11½ inches in the Jeffrey Pine, in the bark which is yellowish-brown in the former and reddish-brown in the latter, and in the foliage which is a deep yellow-green in the former and a dark blue-green in the latter. While both barks are similar, the Jeffrey Pine has an odor of vanilla in its bark crevices.

The only 2-needle pine of the Park, the Lodgepole Pine (*Pinus contorta*), forms extensive forests at elevations of 7,000 to 10,000 feet—indeed, it is so abundant as to be the one plebeian tree of the High Sierra. In general the tree is not more than 2 feet in diameter and 50 feet in height, but much larger specimens may be found. The species may be distinguished by its 2-needle bundles which range in length from 1 to 2½ inches and are generally curved; by its small cones (length ¾ to 2½ inches); and by its thin, flaky, purplish bark.

The only known specimen of the Singleleaf Pinyon (*Pinus monophylla*) in the Park grows on a granite ridge between Tiltill Valley and Rancheria Creek overlooking Hetch Hetchy Reservoir. This grove, the only one in Yosemite National Park, is some two acres in extent and contains about 100 trees. Isolated trees occur on Piute Creek in Muir Gorge and on Rancheria Mountain.

The true firs (genus *Abies*) differ from all their American relatives of the Pine Family by bearing erect cones. But, of all the American firs only two species inhabit Yosemite National Park. The White Fir (*Abies concolor*) is common at elevations from 3,500 to 8,000 feet, and may be seen at numerous places, including Yosemite Valley, Glacier Point, and White Wolf. The California Red Fir (*Abies magnifica*) is found at elevations of 6,000 to 9,000 feet, and extensive forests occur on the Tioga Road and the road to Glacier Point. Both species are beautifully symmetrical with erect, narrow, dense, spire-like crowns and delicate regularly whorled branches. All firs are lovers of shade and therefore usually grow in dense stands crowding out the less tolerant species. The white fir may be identified by its leaves, which are 1 to 2 inches long, without leaf stalks, and flattened or 2-ranked on the lower branchlets; by the bark which in the younger trees is white and bears balsam blisters and in the older trees is deeply furrowed, corky, ashy-gray in color; and by the cones which are 3 to 5 inches in length, and borne erect near the tops of the trees. The California red fir, on the other hand, may be identified by its short needles ¾ to 1½ inches in length which generally curl upward on

Jeffrey Pine seem to prefer solitude and seek out the desolate windswept granite slopes. This one grows on Sentinel Dome. National Park Service photo

the branchlets; by the bark which in the younger trees is silvery-gray but in middle-aged and older trees is a dark-red, or purplish, and divided into small plates; and by the large cones 5 to 8 inches in length, which are borne near the tips of the trees and generally have bracts sticking from between the scales.

The Mountain Hemlock (*Tsuga Mertensiana*) ventures southward from Alaska along the mountain sides, ascending higher and higher until, in Yosemite National Park, it is found only in alpine forests above 9,000 feet elevation. It is universally proclaimed the most graceful tree of the mountains. The beautiful drooping tip and branches set it aside from all other conifers, and its customary bleak surroundings only enhance its graceful charm. The tree may easily be distinguished by its drooping habit; by the short, petioled leaves ½ to ¾ inches in length which clothe the branchlets all around, but sometimes have the appearance of being grouped in star-shaped clusters; and by the small pendulous papery cones (length ½ to 3 inches) which adorn the ends of the branches.

A most interesting small evergreen is the California Torreya (*Torreya californica*), a member of the yew family. There are just five species of *torreya* in the world, one in Japan, two in China, one in Florida, and this one in California, which is restricted to very limited portions of the Sierra Nevada and Coast Ranges. In Yosemite National Park between Arch Rock Entrance Station and The Cascades, the California torreya, often called the California nutmeg, may be seen growing along the Merced road. Some shrublike trees occur along the Big Oak Flat Road below Cascade Creek. Others may be seen near the west portal of the Wawona Tunnel, and near the 5,000 foot elevation along the Wawona Road. A fairly good and representative stand of California torreya exists north of Hetch Hetchy, and the tree occurs in the Mariposa Grove. The foliage of the California torreya is dark-green and its sharp-pointed needle-like leaves which range in length from 1¼ to 2½ inches are flattened in two ranks along the branchlets. When crushed, the foliage gives off a pungent odor. Its fleshy, plum-like cones average about 1½ inches in length, and have a hard-shelled kernel which, when dried, looks much like the nutmeg of commerce.

The Douglas-fir (*Pseudotsuga menziesii*) is the most important timber tree in the world. In Oregon and Washington it forms great forests, but here near the southern limit of its range we find it sparsely mixed with other species of the middle altitudes. There are some splendid old specimens in the cool shade of Yosemite's

118

great south wall and on the talus slopes up to 5,500 feet elevation. The tree is most easily recognized by its medium-sized pendulous cones which are 2 to 4 inches in length and have trident-shaped bracts sticking from between the scales; by its drooping lower branchlets which are clothed all around with petioled leaves from ¾ to 1½ inches in length; and by the thick, deeply furrowed ashy brown bark.

Unlike most conifers, the Western Juniper (*Juniperus occidentalis*) grows on desolate wind-swept slopes, there detached from other species as well as from others of its kind. In such places, it develops grotesque shapes, and becomes picturesque to a degree rarely found in Yosemite trees. Long, exposed roots cling to small cracks at the base of its stocky, gnarled, and widely buttressed trunk. Seldom does it attain any great height, for it is dismembered by snow avalanches, lightning, and fierce winds. The characteristics which easily identify the species are its gnarled form; its thin, stringy, light cinnamon-brown bark; its tiny scale-like leaves which are arranged in whorls of three around the branchlets and are closely pressed to the twigs; and its fruit which is a small blue berry with a sweetish, pungent, aromatic taste. The berries are really modified cones.

The Common Juniper (*Juniperus communis*) also occurs in Yosemite National Park; it is half-prostrate and shrublike, seldom as much as 2 feet high, and grows in the remote high elevations in the northern part of the Park. Instead of the scale-like leaves common to the genus, it has fairly long, needle-like leaves. It will be encountered by few visitors and recognized as a tree by fewer still.

Named for the distinctive and pungent odor of its wood, the Incense-Cedar (*Libocedrus decurrens*) is one of the most abundant conifers in Yosemite Valley and on the talus slopes above. The vivid green of its perfectly formed crown contrasted with its fluted brown trunk make it a constant object of admiration. Chief among the distinguishing characteristics are the flat sprays which are made up of scalelike leaves, the bases of which are closely adherent to the branchlets; the small cones which range from ¾ to 1¼ inches in length and are made up of 5 (apparently 3) scales; and the golden- or cinnamon-brown fibrous bark.

The most famous of all of Yosemite's trees is the Giant Sequoia (*Sequoia gigantea*). This tree, widely known as possibly the oldest and largest living thing, occurs in but 26 groves which are all found at elevations from 4,000 to 8,000 feet in the Sierra Nevada from the vicinity of Lake Tahoe on the north to the region about

Kings River Canyon on the south. There are, of course, three groves in the Park (see Chapter 3). In its natural habitat the tree is seldom confused with any of its associates. Among its distinguishing characteristics are the massive clear trunks with their cinnamon- or chocolate-brown fibrous bark; the closely overlapped leaves which are awl-like on the lower part of the tree and scale-like near the top; and the brilliant brown cones which vary in length from 1½ to 3 inches. Often confused, however, are the Giant Sequoia of the Sierra Nevada and the redwood of the Coast Range, two trees of similar size and fame and with similar reddish bark and wood. Their foliage is a little different, however, and their cones cannot be confused. Certainly, though, their distribution is the best way to distinguish them, for they never occur together. Giant sequoia is called less commonly by other names, including bigtree and Sierra redwood, thus causing more confusion between it and the redwood of the coast. Giant Sequoia and its close relatives, the redwood and bald cypress, had in ages past a much wider distribution. Today the genus *Sequoia* is restricted to California and southwestern Oregon and is represented only by *Sequoia sempervirens* (the redwood of the Coast Range) and *Sequoia gigantea* (the Giant Sequoia of the Sierra Nevada). The following table compares the two species:

Sequoia sempervirens Monterey County to S. Oregon, near the coast		*Sequoia gigantea* West slope Sierra Nevada, between 5,000 and 8,000 feet elevation
300 to 350 feet	Usual height	250 to 300 feet
359 feet	Tallest	324 feet
12 to 20 feet	Usual diameter	15 to 30 feet
1200 to 1800 years	Mature age	2500 to 3500 years or more
Seeds and root sprouts	Reproduction	Seeds only
Single needles like the fir	Foliage	Small, overlapping, awl-shaped needles
Many in pure stands	Associations	Mixed forests with pine and fir

Mariposa Grove, one of the Park's spectacular scenic attractions, contains 200 mature giant sequoias. National Park Service photo

BROAD-LEAVED TREES OF THE PARK

With few exceptions the broad-leaved trees of Yosemite National Park lose their leaves in the fall. This, and its related phenomena, is the result of the tree's preparation for winter. As the season approaches, deciduous trees must necessarily be ready to withstand its rigors. These preparations are largely to prevent excessive transpiration, since abnormal loss of water may result in the death of the tree. They are responsible for the vivid fall colors characteristic of the foliage of many deciduous trees, the annual loss of foliage, and the development of many features useful in winter identification.

When considered along with the cone-bearing trees, the broad-leaved trees of the Park are of comparatively little importance—far less so than would appear from a casual inspection of the oak-dotted floor of Yosemite Valley. As you drive along the approach roads to the Park from the west or up the San Joaquin Valley, you will note both the Interior Live Oak (*Quercus Wislizenii*) and the Blue Oak (*Quercus douglasii*). But, in the Park, both are very rare and are not often found in areas traversed by the average visitor. However, Park visitors should have no difficulty recognizing the California Black Oak (*Quercus Kelloggii*). It is not only one of the most distinctive and beautiful trees in the Park, but in its resemblance to the eastern black oak it possesses many of the characters typical of the oak group with which most people are familiar. Growing best at elevations of 3,000 to 5,000 feet, it is one of the most common trees throughout the canyon of the Merced and in Yosemite Valley. It may easily be distinguished by its large leaves, the deep lobes of which are sharply pointed, and by the dark bark which is deeply checked into small plates.

The talus slopes around and above the Valley floor are the favorite habitat of the Canyon Live Oak (*Quercus chrysolepis*) which may be distinguished by its whitish bark and by its small entire leaves with revolute margins and spiny-toothed leaves on the same twigs, the old leaves being lead-color beneath, and the young leaves yellow powdery beneath. It thrives anywhere from 3,000 to 6,000 feet elevations. Above 5,000 feet one commonly finds the dwarf Huckleberry Oak (*Quercus vaccinifolia*), a shrub 4 to 8 feet high which much resembles the Canyon Live Oak.

Another common tree of the talus slopes is the California Laurel (*Umbellularia californica*). The evergreen, smooth, shiny leaves have a most agreeable camphoric-pungent odor when crushed,

122

and are dried and used for spice. The yellow flowers of early spring develop into yellowish-green, olive-like fruits which mature in autumn. This laurel is usually 20 to 30 feet tall and rarely more than 6 inches in diameter with erect, slender branches forming a loose, open, and narrow crown. It often takes the form of a many-stemmed shrub 10 to 15 feet tall—particularly in moist, shaded locations along streams in protected canyon bottoms. The bark, smooth on young trees and scaly on old trunks, is thin and varies from a dull greenish-brown to reddish-brown in color. Smaller branches are light-green in color.

Of these the tree which excites the most admiration is the Pacific Dogwood (*Cornus Nuttallii*). Although it is occasionally found as high as 7,000 feet it is most generally noted at lower elevations. It is partial to moist, well-drained soils of mountain slopes and protected locations in valley bottoms. One will note it in abundance along the Wawona Road, and along the Big Oak Flat Road, as well as in many sections of Yosemite Valley. In the latter place it can be most readily found about Happy Isles, in the vicinity of Fern Springs, and about the Pohono Bridge. In early spring the showy white flowers (really modified flower-bud scales) appear even before the leaves and often completely cover the crown. In autumn the clusters of bright red fruit and brilliant red, orange, and yellow foliage make it the most beautifully colored of all Yosemite trees.

Along the streams, especially within the Valley, are a number of moisture-loving species. About fifteen species of willow occur within the Park but all except the Pacific Willow (*Salix lasiandra*), Red Willow (*Salix lævigata*), and Scouler Willow (*Salix Scouleriana*). The first-named is perhaps the most common. It can be readily found along the banks of the Merced River in Yosemite Valley. But all willows are deciduous trees or shrubs with simple, alternate leaves. The staminate (male) and pistillate (female) flowers are borne on different trees in narrow, elongated clusters known as catkins. The fruit is a capsule which contains many seeds, each bearing a tuft of hairs at the base, by means of which the seeds are dispersed by the wind. The bark has a bitter, quinine-like flavor. The leaves, which are generally elongated, have a pair of peculiar ear-shaped growths (stipules) at the base of the leaf stems.

The Bigleaf Maple (*Acer macrophyllum*) is abundant in moist shady spots, especially in the shadow of the great south wall of the Valley and in the deep canyon of the Merced at its head. Although it is not exceptionally large as a rule, it is a handsome tree. Mature specimens may attain a maximum of 80 feet in height and 2 to 2½ feet in diameter. When growing in the open the large, heavy branches produce a broad, spreading, round-topped crown densely covered with foliage. The most characteristic feature, however, is large "maple" leaves.

Although this species will be most generally noted as a tall shrub, the Rocky Mountain or Dwarf Maple (*Acer glabrum*) occasionally attains the stature of a small tree, reaching a height of 10 to 15 feet and a diameter of 3 to 4 inches. It generally occurs in moist but poor gravelly-to-rocky soils in protected canyons and gulches up to about the 7,000 foot elevation. Hikers using the Ledge Trail will find it common in such situations along that route. The leaves, borne opposite on the branches, have slender stems 1 to 5 inches long, are 1 to 3 inches across, rather conspicuously veined, and are dark green and shiny upon the upper surface (paler below). They are 3- (occasionally five-) lobed, with the edges of the lobes coarsely toothed. The stems of the leaves are occasionally red.

The Black Cottonwood (*Populus trichocarpa*) is the largest of the Park's poplars—grows up to 125 feet. Although not a tree of particular beauty, it is one of the most easily recognized of the Park's broad-leaved trees. It is rarely found above 4,500 feet and is common in the Yosemite Valley, Wawona, and Hetch Hetchy areas where it grows along streams or in moist meadows. Numbers of fine specimens can be readily found along the Merced River in Yosemite Valley. Several are growing on the bank of Yosemite Creek which borders the cabin area of Yosemite Lodge. Young trees, as well as the branches and upper trunk of mature specimens, are characterized by smooth, pale-gray bark which assumes a dark-gray, heavily ridged and furrowed character on old trunks. The thick, leathery leaves, finely toothed along the edges, are from 2 to 7 inches long, broad at the base and tapering to an acute point. They are shiny green on the upper side, pale to silvery-white beneath, and are further characterized by large, conspicuous veins. Mid-veins, and often the slender round leaf stems, are sometimes slightly hairy.

The small Quaking Aspen (*Populus tremuloides*) is one of the most lovable of all mountain trees. But Park visitors who remain on the Valley floor will not have the pleasure of observing the graceful beauty of this tree for it is found at higher elevations, rarely growing below 5,000 feet. It will be most readily noted

124

along the Tioga Road in the vicinity of Yosemite Creek, on the Glacier Point Road near Bridalveil Creek or in the vicinity of Badger Pass, along the trail between Nevada Falls and Merced Lake, about Washburn Lake, and between Glen Aulin and Water-wheel Falls. Aspen Valley owes its name to the groves of this species in that area. The small delta-shaped leaves which are yellow-green above and silvery beneath are so fastened to their twigs that they tremble with the least breeze. This characteristic, together with the smooth, white bark, make it impossible to confuse the tree with any other species.

The White Alder (*Alnus rhombifolia*) is one of the most common trees of the Transition Zone where it is found in considerable abundance in moist sandy soils bordering streams, up to 4,500 feet in elevation. It is particularly common at Happy Isles, about Mirror Lake, in many places along the banks of the Merced River in Yosemite Valley, while Alder Creek near Wawona owes its name to the abundance of these trees at certain locations along its course. The white alder can be readily identified by its smooth, steel-gray bark (on young trees) which becomes scaly and ridged with age, and the conspicuous, cone-like features—¼ to ½ inch long—which bear the seeds, and which are known as strobiles. The leaves are alternate on the branches, are large (½ to 2 inches wide and from 2 to 3 inches long), a dark lustrous green on the upper surface, ovate in outline with coarsely toothed margins and prominent veins extending to the margins.

The Choke-cherry (*Prunus virginiana*), which is found up to 5,500 feet, is not of great importance in the forests of Yosemite National Park. But its dense, elongated clusters of white flowers, or its fruit, often attract the attention of Park visitors. In rich soil of protected locations it occurs singly or in small groups as a slender, crooked-stemmed tree from 20 to 25 feet tall. In drier, less desirable situations it sometimes forms shrubby thickets 4 to 10 feet tall. Although new twigs are green, the color of older bark is a light reddish-brown to gray, smooth, except on older and larger trunks, in which case it is rough and irregularly seamed with reddish-brown scales. The leaves, which are 1 to 3½ inches long at maturity, are thick, somewhat leathery, and a deep green, being shiny on the upper side and paler beneath. The name choke-cherry is derived from the fact that the fruit has an astringent after-taste.

While the Klamath Plum (*Prunus subcordata*) is usually a shrub, it often reaches a height of from 15 to 20 feet and attains

125

a diameter of from 4 to 6 inches. It does best in sandy, fertile soils along stream borders and similar moist situations. In the Yosemite region it may be noted along the road in the Wawona area, about Big Meadows, and in the Hetch Hetchy section. It is characterized by a short, thick trunk having ashy-brown, seamed bark. The limbs are heavy, extend at right angles from the trunk, and possess numerous short, stubby twigs. In the spring the tree bears white flowers about ½ inch in diameter, which appear just before or at about the same time as the leaves, in loose clusters of 2 to 4. The leaves, when mature, are 1 to 3 inches long, almost circular in outline, and with numerous small teeth along the margin. The fruit is tart but edible, a deep purple-red in color, and about ¾ of an inch to 1 inch long.

The Mountain-mahogany (*Cercocarpis parvifolius*), the California Buckeye (*Aesculus californica*), and the Oregon Ash (*Fraxinus oregona*) are small shrub-like trees of the foothill region. Being generally found in the chaparral areas they enter the Park only in the lower reaches of the great canyons. Specimens have been found in the vicinity of the Arch Rock Entrance and at points along the western Park boundary to Hetch Hetchy.

Visitors to Yosemite National Park will note a number of interesting trees that were planted in the early days before this area became a National Park and which, although they are not native to this area, have been allowed to remain because of their association with the early history of the region. In this category fall the American elm, the black locust, and sugar maple, found in a number of places on the Valley floor, as well as several kinds of fruit trees. The latter are, perhaps, the most conspicuous and best-known of these introduced trees. With few exceptions they are apple trees and, insofar as the Valley is concerned, are contained primarily in three orchards. One of these is included within the parking area near Camp Curry, a second will be noted in the meadow just east of the Yosemite Park and Curry Co. stables, and a third is in the vicinity of the Yosemite Park and Curry Co. utility area near the road between Yosemite Lodge and Government Center.

American elms as well as black locusts will be noted in the Old Village. Trees of the latter species will also be found in the Pioneer Cemetery, in the vicinity of Camp Curry, and along the highway near the start of the Four Mile Trail. The black locusts in the latter place are reminders of the period in Yosemite history when that area was an important public center in the Valley. In

126

addition two sugar maples will be found in the Old Village just east of the general store.

These "outsiders" of the original generation remain among the natives by sufferance. It is the policy of the National Park Service to eliminate, insofar as possible, all exotic (non-native) plants and animals which may gain a foothold in the National Parks, but these living relics of pioneer days in Yosemite Valley may remain until Nature deals the inevitable deathblow. They will not be replaced except by their scattered progeny which may escape the watchful eye of the forester. In time, even the scattered progeny will succumb to Nature's control.

FLOWERING PLANTS OF THE PARK

At least twelve hundred species and varieties of flowering plants may be found within the confines of the Park, and besides these are many lovely ferns and other plants, members of the moss and lichen tribes. In most cases these plants are typical of the Sierra and may be found, in modified form, throughout most of the range; a few, however, are rare and occur only in special locations or restricted areas. The blooming season is long within the Park; during April and May the foothills at the lower borders are radiant with spring flowers—this bloom travels slowly up the slopes and does not reach the high mountains until August, where it remains through September—six months of spring flowers!

Entering the Park by any route that leads up the western slope, one passes through the Chaparral, the foothill zone. The miles upon miles of heavy brush-cover present a similar appearance, and the individual shrubs with spreading crowns, leathery leaves, small flowers, crooked branches, and tough wood look much alike. Yet here are species of oak, manzanita, chamiso (*Adenostoma*), ceanothus and others banded together in an elfin forest that is well-nigh impenetrable and successfully meets the rigors of the foothill region.

One of the most aggressive of these shrubs, the Buck-Brush (*Ceanothus cuneatus*) enters the Park at its lower borders, and one stand of it flourishes on the warm cliffs above Vernal Fall at an altitude of 5,500 feet.

The lower hills have the greatest flower gardens: California Poppy (*Eschscholtzia californica*), Owl's Clover (*Orthocarpus purpurascens*), Innocence (*Collinsia bicolor*), and Sunshine (*Baeria*

127

in several species) spread far and wide the enchantment of their glowing colors.

If one approaches the Park along the Highway Route 120 beside the Merced River, there are several remarkable shrubs growing near the riverbank that claim the attention: The Redbud or Judas Tree (*Cercis occidentalis*) is a bower of rose-purple flowers before the leaf buds unfold, and in the summer this member of the Pea family dangles row upon row of roundish red-green pods from its widespread branches; delightful at all seasons with aromatic stems and leaves, the Sweet-Shrub, Wine Flower or Spice Bush (*Calycanthus occidentalis*) blooms with flowers like small red chrysanthemums, many narrow sepals and petals set upon a cup-like base give this appearance, and the shrub is beloved whereever it grows; with graceful sprays thickly studded with large, white saucer-shaped flowers, the Western Syringa (*Philadelphus Lewisii*) reminds people of a shrub in their gardens that closely resembles this wild plant. Farther up the river other shrubs commence to flower early: the Deer-Bush (*Ceanothus integerrimus*), upon the leaves of which the native mule deer delight to browse, is an ethereal beauty with snowy plumes; with pendulous clusters of almond-scented flowers the choke-cherry is another beauty.

The Mariposa Manzanita (*Arctostaphylos Mariposa*) and the Green Manzanita (*Arctostaphylos patula*) with bright-red bark and smooth green leaves and berries, are here in the Park in small numbers. The manzanitas are among the first to bloom in spring, and March of a good year finds this member of the heath family glorious with the multitudinous clusters of pink bells.

The wood in the vicinity of springs and streams is glorified, during March, by the snowy splendor of the flowers of the Pacific Dogwood (see page 123). The great white "flowers" frequently 4 inches across, resting lightly on the spreading dogwood branches, put one in mind of a flock of white moths. What is spoken of as a flower is really a cluster of flowers, the large white "petals" being modified leaves subtending a cluster of small flowers borne on the central cone-shaped receptacle. Along the streams grows the Creek Dogwood (*Cornus pubescens*). It is a deciduous shrub with red stems that appear very bright in winter when the ground is covered with snow. Another small shrub-like plant is the Western Azalea (*Rhododendron occidentalis*), its delightful clusters of fragrant flowers hang above the white water of the spring streams (especially near Vernal Fall), and it is glorious in the wet El Capitan Meadow, where a pink and yellow variety flourishes.

128

These interesting snowplants (Sarcodes sanguinea) are seen best in June near Glacier Point or in Mariposa Grove. National Park Service photo

In the low meadows of Yosemite Valley early in June are a scattering stand of beautiful Shooting-Stars (*Dodecatheon Jeffreyi*), the White Knotweed (*Polygonum bistortoides*) waves its close head of flowers above the surrounding grasses; Common Larkspur (*Delphinium decorum* var *patens*), Golden Stars (*Brodiæa ixioides*), Death Camas (*Zygadenus elegans*); Sego Lily (*Calochortus Nuttallii*) are represented by small numbers. The wild strawberry (*Fragaria californica*) is rather common in the Sentinel Meadow, where it holds its own better than any other native plant. During July the native meadow plants to appear in flower are the fresh-appearing pink Canchalagua (*Erythraea venusta*); the beautiful Mariposa (*Calochortus venustus*) which appears in a wide range of colors, the form common in the meadow being white and lavender, and forms found along the Big Oak Flat and Wawona Roads varying in color from white to deep-purple and with many bright shades of rosy-lavender in between; Owl's Clover (*Orthocarpus lacerus*); Tansy or Millfoil (*Achillaea lanulosa*); Sneezeweed (*Helenium biglovii*); and a few others, either very rare or small and inconspicuous.

The marshes, of which there are several on the Valley floor, support a delightful growth of large Lady-Ferns (*Athyrium Filixfemina*). These ferns unfold their splendid fronds during June, and this year a scattering of Reinorchis (*Habenaria leucostachys*) and Alpine Lilies (*Erythronium grandiflorum*), lifted their white and yellow flowers about the great garden of green.

A few flowers are left in the drier sections of the Valley that still create a small display; chief among these are Farewell-to-Spring (*Godetia viminea* var. *incerta*), a striking deep-purple flower of 4 petals; *Gilia leptalea* (Branching Gilia), a graceful branching plant with trumpet-shaped flowers of rose-red or lavender; Western Pennyroyal (*Monardella odoratissima*); Lessingia (*Lessingia leptoclada*), a branching plant with scattered heads of lavender flowers, usually described by the visitor as "asters"; and two other members of the sunflower family, Tarweed (Species of *Madia* and others); and Mule Ears or Compass Plant (*Wyethia angustifolia* var. *foliosa*). Mingled with these flowers are the Brake Ferns (*Pteris aquelina*), a fern with a triangular-shaped frond common in all parts of the Valley with the exception of the low meadows.

One of the remarkable sights of the upper reaches of the Valley in midsummer are the fields of tall yellow Evening Primroses (*Œnothera biennis*). They have very handsome large golden flowers which open at twilight and close again in the middle of the following day. In favorable seasons the dry open fields about Yosemite are often yellow with these stately plants. Many of the finest groups, however, are now a thing of the past, due to the mowing of the meadows for wild hay.

Mints of several species grow along the small streams and in damp shaded spots, such as the White Hedge Nettle (*Stachys albans*), a white wooly plant; *Mentha canadensis,* with dense whirls of lavender flowers in the leafaxils; and the introduced Spearmint (*Mentha spicata*). Here, too, are found species of Monkey Flower; the showy ones are the Common Monkey Flower (*Mimulus guttatus*) and the beautiful scarlet Monkey Flower (*Mimulus cardinalis*), is becoming rare on the Valley floor, but is quite common in upland meadows.

Plants of restricted habitat on the Valley floor include the violet family which has five members: *Viola Purpurea* (Yellow Pine Violet) blooms in April and May under the tall ponderosa pines and groves of black oak; at about the same time another yellow violet blooms at the edge of the marshes and along shaded streams, *Viola glabella;* another yellow flowered violet with lobed leaves in the grove of black oaks that fringe the talus at the base of the south wall, while the oak leaves are still in bud; during May the White Violet, sweet *Viola Blanda* may be found in flower in the low meadows and on shady banks; two months later this dainty violet may be found at an altitude of 10,000 feet, fringing the grassy banks of brooks that cut deep channels into the felt-like turf of the alpine meadows; and last to the low meadows comes the Sierra Blue Violet (*Viola adunca*).

Along the roads one may see in May or June the White Mariposa Lily (*Calochortus venustus*). This is one of the handsomest of all mariposas and is remarkable for its range of color. Along the Wawona Road one form has deep wine-red petals which are darker toward the middle and are crossed below by a broad yellow band; still other plants, the more usual form, are nearly white with a dark-brown eye surrounded by yellowish shadings. The Lily family is well represented by many other interesting species. The Tiger or Leopard Lily (*Lilium pardalinum*) occurs in such places as Bridalveil Meadows where as many as twenty-eight flowers have been counted on a single plant. The Little Tiger Lily (*Lilium parvum*) has flowers about half as large and grows in moist meadows at higher elevations. Mahala Mat (*Ceanothus prostratus*) is found in pine forests of the Park.

The high mountain meadows above Yosemite are frequently wonderful wild gardens. Many of the plants that grow in the Valley also grow up here. The streams of this area are often lined with clumps of the Labrador Tea (*Ledum glandulosum*). This is an evergreen shrub with shiny oval leaves which, due to the resin which they contain, are peculiarly fragrant when crushed. The white flowers are grouped at the ends of the branches in flat-topped clusters. By the stream bed one may often find lovely robust plants of the large Pink Monkey Flower (*Mimulus Lewisii*) which replaces the scarlet species of the Yosemite and lower valleys. The flowers are showy, light-pink, and plainly two-lipped but the two lips are similar. In these swamps grow the quaint Elephant Heads (*Pedicularis grœnlandica*) with its slender rose-pink spikes. The name Elephant Heads arises from the peculiar corolla with its hooded upper lip prolonged into a curved beak or proboscis. Associated with the foregoing one finds the blue Whorled Pentstemon (*Pentstemon confertus*) which is not so tall nor so many flowered as that at lower altitudes. Often a marshy stretch may be covered with the pale creamy cups of the Marsh Marigold (*Caltha biflora*). The Western Wallflower (*Erysimum asperum*) with its pretty blossom is quite common, too.

The different meadows often vary greatly in their plant composition. On the one hand one may see meadows filled with flowers that grow higher than the waist and so thickly that it is impossible to step without treading down many plants. There are Rein Orchis (*Habenaria unalaschensis*) with long tresses of small white flowers; many species of Lupins, the largest and most attractive of which bears great masses of showy Blue Spikes (*Lupinus longipes*); the great yellow Coneflower (*Rudbeckia californica*) standing shoulder-high and ending in a single conical head; the purple Fireweed (*Epilobium angustifolium*) which raises its long wands to the breeze; and the curious Corn Lily (*Veratrum californicum*) which adds its characteristic large-leafed clumps and stout corn-like stems to the meadow population, recalling in its appearance the Eastern False Hellebore. Instead of these rank growing meadows one may see a close carpet of green painted here and there with brilliant patches of crimson, gold, and pale lavender. The crimson on closer observation proves to be the bright crimson Indian Paintbrush (*Castilleja californica*), the gold Potentilla (*Potentilla Gordonii*), and the lavender the Mountain Daisy (*Erigeron compositus*).

The swampy alpine meadows of the Subalpine Belt (at about

132

9,000 to 10,000 feet) often possess an interesting inhabitant of the Heath Family. The little Kalmia (*Kalmia polifolia* var. *microphylla*) with its curious pink bloom carrying the anthers in pockets of the corolla, is always a quest with the climbers who know rare plants. If one watches these meadows carefully he will see the tiny pink or white bells of the Dwarf Bilberry (*Vaccinium cæspitosum*) close against the ground. On gentle slopes moist with seepage water from the snowbanks above, one finds the Snow Fairies (*Lewisia pygmæa*), tiny plants with a few white star-flowers. Two other diminutive shrubs of the Heath Family also grow at these high altitudes. The Red Heather (*Bryanthus Breweri*) has stems densely clothed with linear leaves and ending in a cluster of red flowers with conspicuous darker-red stamens; it has the greater altitudinal range of the two heathers and is often quite abundant. The White Heather Bell (*Cassiope Mertensiana*) is usually found with the red heather at the higher altitudes; it grows in heavy masses along the Lyell Fork of the Tuolumne and picturesquely decorates the margins of most high mountain lakes.

The flora of the Sierra Nevada comprise one of the most marked and distinct units of vegetation of the earth's surface. The Yosemite National Park area is thoroughly typical of it, and not elsewhere on the Sierra chain can a transection of it be studied to better advantage than here. All the flowering formations are remarkable, and each in its best seasons has its own peculiar interests. This fact is singularly true because primitive conditions prevail over most of the area, and even in the foothills undisturbed plant societies may still be found by the explorer; while within the Park limits the native plantlife still reflects the old-time glory of the natural gardens of the Sierras.

Remember that in a National Park, destruction, defacement, or removal of trees, or rocks, is prohibited as is the picking or carrying away of flowers or plants.

A black-tailed deer (O.h. Columbianus).
National Park Service photo

Chapter 6.

Wildlife of the Park

YOSEMITE NATIONAL PARK, aside from its scenic and plant grandeur, offers a large, varied, and interesting complement of
animal life. This is partially explained by the variety of living conditions here as, for example, the great range in elevation (2,000
to 13,000 feet). Another reason is the policy of protection for all
native living things in National Parks. This serves to assure present-
day visitors the privilege of enjoying them and it predicates that
future generations may also be able to enjoy a remnant of the
Sierran wilderness with its coincident wildlife.

A number of the Park's wild animals can be seen and enjoyed by
the visitor who seeks them in a proper fashion. Animals that have
never known trap or gun are relatively unafraid of humans. Of
course, you cannot expect to see all the species reported to live in
the Park. Some forms of wildlife are quite rare here. Many are
difficult to identify in the field. Others are abroad mainly at night.
Still others are rarely surprised above ground. However, cultivat-
ing the "seeing eye," being alert as you travel the roads and trails,
will prove rewarding.

In all National Parks, the policy of maintaining an area as a
wilderness zone just as it would operate naturally, with as little
artificial interference as possible, is the goal to be achieved. Thus
the Park Service limits road building and all types of construction
to a minimum, allowing just enough artificial disturbance so that
you may enter the area and see the way Nature is caring for its
own and has been doing so for hundreds of years. In all nature
there is what is called a biotic balance: a balance between different
species of animals, and between animals and plantlife within an

135

area. Briefly, as an example, it might be said that although many deer are killed each year by predators such as coyotes or cougars, the Park Service does not try to eliminate the predator, or interfere in any way in its pursuit of food and shelter, realizing that if they were to eliminate all predators of one species such as deer, the deer would increase in abundance above all capacity of the range to support them. Furthermore, the weak and diseased members of the deer population, the individuals most vulnerable to predators, would be more likely to survive and to compete with healthy individuals for the available food.

As a whole the Park Service interferes very little with the normal lives of the animals within the Park. You may help them to keep the biotic balance by not feeding the bears, because when bears expect handouts from humans and depend on such for their food, they gradually become dangerous and pestiferous, as well as less healthy, and rangers sometimes have to trap such bears, removing them from the area, or sometimes disposing of them by shooting. Generally speaking, all wild animals will be much more healthy if they are left to forage for themselves rather than depending on man for their proper nutritive balance. Fires also upset the biotic balance and destroy homes for wildlife, as well as animals themselves. Therefore, be careful with smokes, matches, and campfires while in the Park.

The most difficult enemy in the Park for an animal to cope with is the automobile. A great many of the squirrels are destroyed by speeding cars, and some of the larger animals are not immune, especially at night when the glare from the headlights of an approaching car seems to blind the animals and cause them to leap in front of the automobile.

MAMMALS OF THE PARK

Mammals are warm-blooded vertebrates with hair or fur, which nourish their young with milk. Yosemite National Park possesses an abundant population of mammals both as to species and individuals.

EVEN-TOED, HOOFED MAMMALS—
Order *Artiodactyla*

The present-day native hoofed mammals of Yosemite are all even-toed, that is, they have two hoofs in contact with the ground on each foot, and may be called cloven-hoofed. Most of the cloven-hoofed mammals of the world have some kind of horns (as in bison or cattle) or antlers (as in deer) for protection or for fighting, in one or both sexes.

MULE DEER (*Odocoileus hemionus*). Yosemite National Park is a meeting ground for three subspecies—the Rocky Mountain mule (*O. h. hemionus*), California (*O. h. californicus*), and Columbian black-tailed deer (*O. h. columbiana*). In Yosemite, it is not always possible to rely on field identification of deer; thus Park naturalists usually refer to the deer of the Park as California mule deer, although certain individuals show some features of the other two forms.

The characteristics of the mule deer are long ears, stiff-legged gait, especially the peg-leg lope, or "buck-jump," when frightened. The young, frequently two, but sometimes only one, are born between June 15 and July 15. Deer are browsing animals, eating chiefly leaves and tender twigs of brush and trees, but they also eat considerable grass and herbs. The bucks have antlers which grow out and are shed every year. Shedding occurs late in January or February, and the new antlers start growing at once. While growing they are covered with a thick, hairy skin called velvet, which is generally shed in September. They are then polished on trees and brush in preparation for the mating season which starts in November. A buck with single point on each side is called a spike; with two on either side a forked-horn; three a three-point, etc. Spikes and forked-horns may be one or two years old respectively, but the number of points does not necessarily indicate the age of the buck. Deer are very common in the Park and range, singly or in small bands, chiefly between altitudes of 3,500 and 8,500 feet in summer and keep below level of deep snow in winter, preferring chaparral country.

Mule deer are the only hoofed mammals in the Park today. Sierra Bighorns (*Ovis canadensis sierrae*) once lived in the higher parts of what is now Yosemite National Park. However, the Park was created too late to save enough of the "mountain sheep" from the larders of the hunter, sheepherder, and miner. They are now all gone.

FLESH-EATERS—Order *Carnivora*

The flesh-eating or predatory mammals are among the best-known animals in the Park.

SIERRA BLACK BEAR
(*Ursus americanus californiensis*)

There is only one species of bear in the Park now, all Grizzlies (*Ursus horribilis*) having been killed many years ago. The black bear varies in color from light yellow through the browns to black. Cubs of varying color may be found in the same litter. These cubs are born during the mother bear's long winter nap. They weigh only 8 to 10 ounces at birth in sharp contrast to the 300 to 500 pounds they attain in adulthood. Usually, twins are born, but sometimes there are triplets. By spring the cubs are ready to travel and join their mother in their feasts on fresh or decaying meat, grasses, berries, honey, insects, or whatever is at hand at the moment. However, it is dangerous and prohibited to feed or molest the bear, and a mother bear with cubs may be a very ferocious beast. Bears are fairly common in the Park.

CALIFORNIA MOUNTAIN LION
(*Felis concolor californica*)

A large cat-like animal that has a body about 5 feet long and rope-like tail 2½ feet long. There are two color phases; one is reddish-brown above, white under, and dark feet, nose, and ears. In the other phase, the body is uniformly tawny or grayish-brown. A full-grown lion, or cougar as it is often called, weighs between 100 and 135 pounds. Their tracks are cat-like, wider than long, between 3½ and 4½ inches across, the heel-pad wide. Young, usually 2 or 3 in number, are born in April and are about the size of a large house cat. Food of the lion consists largely of deer. They are said to kill about one each week. Lions are among the most shy and retiring animals in the Park, seldom seen, not at all dangerous to human beings, and vital in the prevention of deer overpopulations. They have been seen along the Wawona Road, in Yosemite Valley, and near Mather Ranger Station. Sometimes tracks are found near Mirror Lake.

CALIFORNIA WILDCAT (*Felis rufus californica*)

This mammal is about twice the size of an average house cat, between 20 and 30 inches long, short stubby tail, long legs. Color reddish brown in summer and gray in winter. Tracks round, and about 2 inches in diameter, sole pad not triangular as in coyote.

ABOVE: *California mountain lion (Felis concolor californica)*. BE-LOW: *Sierra black bear (Ursus americanus californiensis)*. National Park Service photos

When walking, hind foot is placed exactly in the track of the front foot on the same side. Young numbering usually about 4, are born late in the spring. They live on small mammals such as squirrels and mice, rarely on quail. They are common in the Park.

MOUNTAIN COYOTE (*Canis latrans lestes*)

It is about the size and general appearance of a small police dog; general color grayish with some reddish on nose and throat; some have black on back. Weight about 25 to 30 pounds. These animals range to the upper timberline and live primarily on small mammals but occasionally kill fawns, and in the winter when the snow is soft may kill full-grown deer. Their tracks are the same as a medium-sized dog's. During the fall and winter, one frequently hears their high-pitched, rapid-series of barks followed by shrill wails. The young number as many as 14 to a litter. They are common in the Park. In winter, they are most numerous in Yosemite Valley, presumably because deep snow reduces the availability of food up high. However, some are at Tuolumne Meadows all winter.

TOWNSEND GRAY FOX
(*Urocyon cinereoagenteus townsendi*)

This small gray fox has a reddish-brown face, a black stripe down its back to tip of its tail, yellowish brown on its sides and legs, and a bush tail. Their common note is a sharp bark. The young, from 3 to 5, are born in a den in the rock or in a hollow tree, are blind, and blackish in color, being entirely different from their adults. They are omnivorous, feeding on gophers, mice, ground-squirrels, rabbits, acorns, berries, and insects. Tracks are like a small dog's and are usually in a straight line. They generally travel at a trot. They are common in the middle and lower elevations of the Park. At night, the car headlights will often pick one up as it scurries away. The first impression may be that it is a cat, for the gray fox is slender and quick.

While the gray fox is common, the Sierra Red Fox (*Vulpes fulva necator*) is a rarity. The gray fox is often mistaken for this species because of certain reddish portions of its coat. The upper-parts of the red fox are a yellowish red and it has a large, bushy tail with a white tip.

140

CALIFORNIA RACCOON (*Procyon lotor psora*)

This animal, sometimes called a "coon," is dark-gray in color and has a short, club-like tail marked with alternating gray and black rings. A black band resembling a mask crosses the face. Hind feet rest flat on the ground like a bear's. Tracks resemble a very small child's. It uses its front paws very dexterously. Coons live along streams where they often make trails while patrolling for their food. They are omnivorous, eating frogs, fish, insects, fruit, berries, nuts, etc. Young, numbering from 4 to 6, are born in a nest in a hollow tree in the spring. They are nocturnal in habit but are occasionally seen in the late afternoon. Though uncommon, they are occasionally observed in Yosemite Valley. However, coons are seen more frequently at Wawona and the South Entrance.

CALIFORNIA RING-TAILED CAT
(*Bassariscus astutus raptor*)

A ringtail has a general light-brown color with white under surface, a tail bushy and marked alternately in rings of gray and black, like a coon's; however, the tail is proportionately longer. Legs are short, body long and slender; slightly longer than a gray squirrel (see page 146). It has a beautifully formed head, large eyes, and intelligent expression. They are strictly nocturnal and seldom seen in daylight. Their food consists of mice, birds, insects, nuts, and berries. Young, numbering 3 to 4, are born in the late spring in a nest in caves, hollow logs, and frequently in buildings. Despite the name, it is *not* closely related to the cat family. It is commonly found at the lower elevations of the Park.

CALIFORNIA BADGER (*Taxidea taxus neglecta*)

Watch for this animal in the open country of the higher elevations. In such locations, it finds a supply of small rodents available for food, where the digging is easy. This grayish-yellow grizzled mammal is well adapted for going underground, with very strong claws and powerful muscles. When waddling along, it appears almost like a turtle, but the narrow white streak along the center of the head and neck are quite striking. The scent emitted by a badger is not especially rank.

CALIFORNIA RIVER OTTER
(*Lutra canadensis brevipilosus*)

It is dark-brown in color and runs from 3½ to 4 feet in length. Otters are well suited to life in the water, with all four feet webbed and the body streamlined. They swim well enough to catch fish and frogs for food. On land, they have a "loping" gait, arching the body greatly. Uncommon, they may appear at lakes in the northwest part of the Park.

NORTHERN CALIFORNIA STRIPED SKUNK
(*Mephitis mephitis occidentalis*)

Its color is black except for a white line on its face, and two white lines down the sides of its back and some white on its tail. The body is chunky, slightly smaller than a coon. They are omnivorous, eating insects, small birds, rodents, frogs, fish, and fruit and berries. They make their dens in many kinds of places; and the young, numbering from 4 to 10, are born in April or May. They are unafraid of man and very slow in getting out of the way. Beware! The skunk emits a strong odor when frightened or provoked. The striped skunk is fairly common in the Park.

CALIFORNIA SPOTTED SKUNK
(*Spilogale gracilis phenax*)

This skunk is much smaller than its striped cousin—about the size of a ground squirrel (see page 147). Its body has irregular short stripes and spots of white, and the end of its tail is white. They are commonly called civet cats. Both skunks belong to the weasel family. Their food consists of small rodents, insects, and fruit. From 2 to 6 young reproduced in May. When approached too closely they have an odd habit of standing on their front feet with their hind quarters in the air; in this way they can pivot and use their characteristic scent glands at the base of the tail to good advantage. Uncommon in the Park.

There are several other members of the weasel family in the Sierra of the Yosemite region. They will be recognized at once as among the important "fur-bearing" species. About the buildings in Yosemite Valley and around rock slides in the higher mountains the Mountain Weasel (*Mustela frenata nevadensis*) occurs in considerable numbers. Its body is long and slender, about 9 to 11

142

ABOVE: *California coon (Procyon lotor psora)*. BELOW: *Northern California striped skunk (Mephitis mephitis occidentalis)*. National Park Service photos

inches long. Its color is brown above and rich yellow below; the tip of its tail is black, in winter the body is solid white except for black tip of the tail. The Sierra Short-tailed Weasel (*Mustela erminea murica*) is smaller than the mountain weasel, up to 8 inches long. While the coloration is similar, this weasel, often called the ermine, ranges from the red fir forest above the rim of the Valley to the rock slides at timberline. Another member of the family that has the same range is Sierra Pine Marten (*Martes americana sierrae*). Slender in form, it is about the size of a small house cat, rich brown on the upper surface, paler beneath, while the end of tail is black; there is a buff or orange spot on its throat. While it resembles the weasel in form of body, it does not change to white in winter. The martens are not common in the Park, and being partially nocturnal, are seldom seen. The Pacific Mink (*Mustela vison energumenos*) is also considered a rare member of Yosemite's weasel family. Slightly larger than a marten, it is a very dark brown in summer, and white in winter. Mink are generally found in or near water, at the lower elevations.

The Pacific Fisher (*Martes pennanti pacifica*) is a long-bodied, short-legged animal like other members of the weasel family, but is about twice the size of a house cat. About 3 to 3½ feet long, it is a blackish-brown with a grizzled effect on the back of the head, shoulders, and along the sides. Often, there is an irregular white spot on the chest. While rare in Yosemite, it ranges from the red fir belt on up to the higher country. But the largest and rarest of the weasel tribe is the Southern Wolverine (*Gulo luscus luteus*). It is a low, squat heavy-bodied animal with short, powerful legs; feet have long claws; and it is about 3½ feet in length, and weighs about 20 pounds. Its color is dark-brown, with yellowish strips across head, face, and from the front legs to the base of tail. Wolverines are powerful, formidable beasts, afraid of nothing except men, and even bears will give them a clear road. They are found at high elevations in very small numbers. Actually, this rare animal is making a last stand in the National Parks of this country and Canada.

RABBITS AND THEIR ALLIES
Order *Lagomorpha*

There are four members of this order to be found in Yosemite National Park.

BLACK-TAILED JACK RABBIT
(*Lepus californicus*)

This animal, also called the California jack rabbit, is the commonest jack seen in the West. In recent years, it has entered the extreme western part of the Park, near Crane Flat and Mather. It can easily be distinguished by the black upper surface of the tail and its very slender body.

WHITE-TAILED JACK RABBIT
(*Lepus townsendi*)

Also called a Sierra hare, it is larger and heavier than the black-tailed jack rabbit; its general color is brown in summer, and white in winter. The feet are heavily covered with fur throughout the year. Uncommon in the Park, it seems to prefer rather flat, sparsely wooded terrain having some bushes present for thick cover, and ranges from 7,000 feet to over 12,000 feet in elevation. Mariposa Brush Rabbit (*Sylvilagus bachmani mariposae*). It is similar in appearance to the well-known cottontail, but with very much less "cotton." It is about half the size of the black-tailed jack rabbit, but with ears shorter in comparison to the body. It is common in the chaparrel of the foothills along the west boundary of the Park, but only a few have been seen within the Park itself.

YOSEMITE CONY (*Ochotona princeps muiri*)

Resembling a small rabbit with short ears, this animal—often called the Sierra Pika—has a general gray color with black tips on the rounded ears and nose. They are found in rock slides at high elevations; their color is very protective and they are seldom seen, although they are rather numerous in the Park. They utter a thin, nasal "eenk, eenk" when excited. Grasses, plant stalks, and seeds form their food. They do not hibernate, but cut hay and store it under rocks for winter use. They usually have two or more litters of 3 or 4 young during the summer.

RODENTS OR GNAWING MAMMALS
Order *Rodentia*

The rodent group is the largest one in the Park. Its members far outnumber any other order.

145

THE SQUIRREL FAMILY (*Sciuridae*)

The California Gray Squirrel (*Sciurus griseus*) will be one of the first mammals to attract the attention of the visitor to Yosemite, for it is commonly found in the Park at elevations up to 7,000 feet. Its body is uniform gray above with whitish underparts. It has a long and bushy tail. The gray squirrel is active practically throughout the year, so that visitors at whatever season will see the species; however, more individuals are out in good weather than during times of heavy snows.

In the forests at 6,000 to 10,500 feet lives the Sierra Chickaree (*Tamiasciurus douglasi albolimbatus*), a "red" squirrel similar in general habits to the gray squirrel but of smaller size and different coloration. The chickaree, or Douglas Squirrel, as it is sometimes called, is dark-brown tinged with reddish on the upper surface, has a black line along each side of the body, and the lower surface of the body is white or buffy white. Its body is about 8 inches long and the moderately bushy tail 5 or 6 inches. The mode of life of the chickaree is similar to that of the gray squirrel. Common in the Park, it is a dweller in the trees and comes to the ground only when necessary to retrieve a fallen cone or to cross an opening not bridged by overhead branches. Where trees are close together as in many parts of the lodgepole pine forest the chickaree literally lives in the trees.

There are five species of small striped chipmunks within the Park boundaries. All agree in general pattern of markings, having the head and back marked with alternate stripes of dark and light color and with more or less bright-brown along the sides, but each species of chipmunk has a definite general range and a particular "niche" within this range; no two species are found in exactly the same surroundings. On the west slope of the mountains in portions of the Foothill and Yellow Pine Belts containing mixed chaparral and trees there is the Merriam Chipmunk (*Eutamias merriami*) a large dark-grayish species. It is found in small numbers in thickets along the north and south walls of Yosemite Valley. The most widely distributed and commonest species of the Yosemite region is the Tahoe Chipmunk (*Eutamias speciosus frater*) which occurs throughout the Lodgepole-Fir and Subalpine Belts. It may be known at once by its small size (total length about 8 inches), bright highly contrasted pattern of coloration, extremely lively manner, and especially by its habit of seeking safety high in the trees, rather than in logs, thickets, or rock heaps.

146

Pack rat (genus Cricetidae)

Sierra golden-mantled ground squirrel (Citellus lateralis chrysodeirus)

California badger (Lutra canadensis brevipilosus). All photographs from National Park Service

Tahoe chipmunks have been seen fifty feet or more above the ground, while none of the other species in the high mountains goes much if any over five feet from the ground. The Lodgepole-Fir Belt possesses also a rather large species of predominantly grayish coloration, the Allen Chipmunk (*Eutamias townsendi senex*). This one lives about boulders, fallen logs, and brush patches. In the upper part of the Yellow Pine Belt and the lower portion of the Canadian, there is a species of about the same size and practically the same habits as the preceding, but with much taller ears and a conspicuous white spot at the hinder base of each ear. This is the Long-eared Chipmunk (*Eutamias quadrimaculatus*), almost as brightly colored as the Tahoe chipmunk. The smallest and palest-colored species within the Park is the Alpine Chipmunk (*Eutamias alpinus*) which dwells among rocks and fallen trees in the Subalpine Belt. It is the timberline chipmunk, the last to be seen during an ascent of Mount Lyell or any of the other loftier summits. All of the chipmunks living above the snow-line (about 3,300 feet) in the Park take a winter "sleep" for longer or shorter periods of time in winter.

There is one member of the squirrel tribe which is observed by very few Yosemite National Park visitors. This is the strictly nocturnal Sierra Flying Squirrel (*Glaucomys sabrinus lascivus*), which is fairly common in the Park. Its general color is dark-gray above, dull-white below, with fur-covered skin between front and hind legs on each side. The tail is flat and heavily furred; the body is about the size of a rat and the eyes are large. While these squirrels *cannot* fly, they can glide for rather long distances, and are able to control their movements from side to side and to some extent upwards. They are active generally throughout the winter.

All of the members of the squirrel family mentioned in the preceding paragraphs are species that live and find shelter chiefly or entirely in trees or logs; but there are also important members of the group which dwell upon and beneath the ground. These are the ground squirrels and the marmot. The Sierra Ground Squirrel (*Citellus beecheyi sierrae*), has brown coloration with whitish shoulders, is in its habits the western counterpart of the Prairie Dog and is found, in the Yosemite region, from the San Joaquin Valley up to an altitude of 8,200 feet in the mountains. In the Lodgepole-Fir and Subalpine Belts is the Sierra Golden-mantled Ground Squirrel (*Citellus lateralis chrysodeirus*), locally called "copperhead." This species has the head and shoulders golden-yellow while the body is marked along each side with two

148

jet-black stripes enclosing one of pure white. The "niche" of this species is in the open forest about bases of large trees and rocks. The Subalpine Belt supports another burrowing species, the Belding Ground Squirrel (*Citellus beldingi*), a rather plainly garbed animal of yellowish-brown coloration and with a reddish wash along the back. It lives altogether in the meadows where it finds abundant forage during the summer months and where it may often be seen sitting up in characteristically erect posture on the lookout for danger. The golden-mantled and Belding ground squirrels hibernate regularly and so do those representatives of the California ground squirrel which live in the Yellow Pine and Lodgepole-Fir Belt where snow lies on the ground during the winter months. All of these rodents feed to repletion during the summer and by fall their bodies are heavily stocked with fat which then serves to warm and nourish them during the long winter sleep.

The Southern Sierra Marmot (*Marmota flaviventer sierrae*), often called "Woodchuck," is the largest local representative of the squirrel family in the Yosemite region. In bodily configuration the marmot is stouter than the other members of the family, with proportionately shorter legs and tail. It is not infrequently mistaken for the badger, a totally different animal which, however, often lives in the same sort of country. Adult marmots measure 15 to 18 inches (head and body), with the tail 5 to 8 inches long, while the weight ranges from 4 to 6½ pounds with different individuals. Here in the Sierras the marmot is a high-mountain animal, dwelling chiefly in the Subalpine Belt. The winter months (from about October until May) are spent in hibernation. They are common in the Park.

YELLOW-HAIRED PORCUPINE
(*Erethizon dorsatum epixanthum*)

Larger than the marmot, it weighs about 15 pounds and its general color is brownish-black, with yellow quills with black tips. The underparts lack quills. Incidentally, the quills are very effective, and the porcupine is unafraid and slow to move. While a "porky" cannot shoot its quills, the black, barbed outer tips of the yellow quills fasten themselves very easily into an "enemy" on contact or may be driven in firmly by the action of the thick muscular tail. Porcupines are common from the lowest reaches of the Park up to more than 10,000 feet and they are active throughout the year.

APLODONTIA (*Aplodontia rufa california*)

This animal, often called a Sierra Mountain Beaver, looks much like a tailless muskrat or a gigantic meadow mouse, blackish-brown in color. It will seldom be seen by the Park visitor, for it utilizes extensive tunnels safely to reach food above ground and is chiefly nocturnal. The burrowings, six or seven inches in diameter, running parallel to the surface, roofless in spots, may be found on bottom land near streams in widely scattered locations at elevations ranging from less than 4,000 feet to more than 10,000 feet.

While not native to the Park, the Golden Beaver (*Castor canadensis subauratus*)—a true member of the beaver species—may be found near the South Entrance and around the stream by the golf course along the Wawona Road. In 1944, the California Division of Fish and Game introduced several colonies at sites along the Big Creek, just south of the Park. Many of these "true" beavers made their way into Yosemite National Park without paying the entrance fee and even decided to make their home here. These beavers attain a length of nearly 4 feet and weight of around 40 pounds. The overall color is a golden-brown, although this may not be readily apparent when the animal is seen at twilight, the fur wet from swimming.

POCKET GOPHERS (*Thomomys*)

There are three kinds of pocket gophers found in the Park. Since they spend most of their lives underground, gophers are seldom seen by Park visitors. Yosemite's species, however, are from light to dark-brown in color, with head and body some 6 inches long, plus a tail of about the proportions of a matchstick, bare at the end. With this bare tip the gopher can feel any obstruction that may be in the way when it needs to back up in a tunnel. Its prominent chisel-teeth always show; the lips do not cover them. The gopher has a heavy head and broad face and its eyes and ears are small. The gopher's fur is short and smooth. When digging, it puts the soil out through a hole temporarily opened on the surface.

MICE AND RATS (*Cricetidae*)

There is a surprisingly large population of mice and rats, the presence of which can hardly be surmised by the casual observer.

150

Intensive trapping shows that rock crevices, old logs, brush heaps, and the like are tenanted by large numbers of White-footed Mice of several species, all agile long-tailed rodents; the grassy meadows everywhere are the homes of chunkily built Meadow Mice with short legs and soft furry coats; and the higher meadows support many of the long-tailed long-legged Jumping Mice. In the rock slides of the higher mountains there lives the much larger Bushy-tailed Wood Rat. This animal, like its smooth-tailed house-building relative in the foothills, is commonly called "pack rat" or "trade rat" because of its habit of carrying away articles of camp equipment and often leaving in their places chips of wood, or other similar tokens. The bushy-tail lives in the rock slides of the Sub-alpine Belt, along with the Yosemite cony and Sierra pine marten. The wood rats exhibit some tendency toward house-building as is shown by the accumulations of twigs and sticks in some of the rock crevices, but the animals rarely do as much in this direction as the Streator Wood Rats in the Foothill Belt. There are better than a dozen known species of mice and rats in Yosemite National Park.

BATS—Order *Chiroptera*

Bats are present in most of the areas of the Park, whence at least fourteen species are known. Certain species are restricted to the warmer valley and foothills, others occur over the floor of the Yosemite gorge, and one species has been found at 10,350 feet altitude near Vogelsang Lake, almost the highest altitudinal record for any species of bat in the United States. In size the Yosemite species range from the tiny Merriam Canyon Bat, which is less than 3 inches long with a total wingspread of less than 8 inches, to the California Mastiff Bat, with a total length of 6½ inches and a wingspread of 19 inches. This is the largest species in the United States. All bats found here are insect-eaters.

Bats are the only mammals capable of *true* flight. Although possessing a wing-like structure, the bat does not have a wing in the sense that a bird has. The "wing" consists of a much modified hand with very long fingers. This is covered with a thin, but very tough membrane, that enables the animal to fly. When at rest, the Bat's wing can be folded up, much as an umbrella closes.

151

MOLES AND SHREWS—Order *Insectivora*

Shrews are the smallest mammals found in the Park, with only the Merriam Canyon bat as a possible rival. Four of the five species found here are less than half the size of a house mouse, have small feet and are some shade of brown. The exception is the mountain water shrew, which is about the size of a house mouse. All five have sharp, pointed noses and tiny eyes. Again excepting the water shrew (because of its size), they can be identified as to species only by the expert who has the specimen in hand.

In Yosemite National Park, shrews generally seem to prefer moist situations and tend to keep under cover, such as matted vegetation, logs, and rocks. The runs and burrows of other mammals are often used as highways in the relentless search for food. While seldom seen by visitors, they have been found at all elevations in the Park and apparently are active in winter as well as summer.

The Yosemite Mole (*Scapanus latimanus sericatus*) is well suited for life underground. The pointed nose, tapered head, short neck, cylindrical body, and lack of protruding ears contribute to smooth passage through loose soil or open tunnel. The short, sturdy front legs with spade-like feet, turned sidewise and equipped with strong, thick nails, form a powerful digging apparatus. A mole can dig itself out of sight before your very eyes, seeming to melt into the earth! The fur is short, thick and reversible as to "lay," so it is not rubbed the wrong way whether the animal is traveling forward or backward. The mouth is placed well on the under side, which would tend to keep dirt out when the animal is digging. Moles have eyes, but they are small and not well developed. The mole pushes excavated soil up through a mound.

BIRDS OF THE PARK

Birds are a continual source of interest to people living close to nature and their study is an interesting hobby for anyone interested in the out-of-doors. As with many of the animals in Yosemite, birds have come to regard man as a relatively harmless feature of their environment and therefore go about seeking their food, building nests and rearing their young with a minimum of diversion due to his presence. This results in a most favorable situation for one who would study the birds, for it often allows close approach and detailed observation of birds with little alteration of their behavior.

For bird watching, binoculars will be found useful. Yosemite National Park's bird population includes over 220 species. The following list of birds of the Park is based almost entirely on reported observations by members of the National Park Service and visiting ornithologists. Status refers to the time and duration of occupancy of an area—whether the bird is present throughout the year (R.—resident), during the winter period only (W. V.—winter visitant), during the summer only (S. V.—summer visitant), or sporadically for brief periods (C. V.—casual visitant). In the latter category are birds that pass through the area only in fall and spring migration or enter it during postbreeding upmountain movements (M.—migrant). The common species names used in this list are in accordance with *Birds of Yosemite National Park* by Cyril A. Stebbins and Robert C. Stebbins. (It also conforms to *A. O. U. Checklist of North American Birds,* 5th edition.) If you have any doubts or questions as to the possibility of a certain species of bird, discuss the matter with one of the Park Naturalists. Remember that the study of birds, as with all animals, calls for great patience, just a reasonable amount of caution, and, of course, common sense.

Abbreviations for Life Zone	*Abbreviations for Status*
F—Foothill or Digger Pine-Chaparral Belt	R—Resident
Y—Yellow Pine Belt	WV—Winter Visitant
L—Lodgepole Pine-Red Fir Belt	SV—Summer Visitant
S—Subalpine	CV—Casual Visitant
A—Alpine Belt	M—Migrant

Loon Family

Arctic Loon–CV

Grebe Family

Eared Grebe–CV
Western Grebe–CV
Pied-billed Grebe–WV

Pelican Family

White Pelican–M

Cormorant Family

Double-crested Cormorant–CV

Heron Family

Great Blue Heron–CV
Green Heron–CV
Common Egret–CV
Snowy Egret–CV
Black-crowned Night Heron–CV

Waterfowl Family

Canada Goose–C
Mallard–CV
Pintail–CV
Green-winged Teal–CV
Blue–winged Teal-CV

(*Continued*)

Waterfowl Family (Cont.)

Cinnamon Teal–CV
American Widgeon–CV
Shoveler–CV
Wood Duck–CV
Redhead–CV
Ring-necked Duck–CV
Canvasback–CV
Lesser Scaup–CV
Common Goldeneye–CV
Barrow's Goldeneye–CV
Bufflehead–CV
Harlequin Duck–CV
Ruddy Duck–CV
Hooded Merganser–SV & CV
Common Merganser–CV

Vulture Family

Turkey Vulture–R; F-S

Hawk Family

White-tailed Kite–CV
Goshawk–R
Sharp-shinned Hawk–R; F-Y
Cooper's Hawk–R; F-Y
Red-tailed Hawk–R; F-S
Swainson's Hawk–SV
Ferruginous Hawk–CV
Golden Eagle–R; F-Y
Bald Eagle–R; F
Marsh Hawk–CV; F-L

Osprey Family

Osprey–CV

Falcon Family

Prairie Falcon–CV
Peregrine Falcon–CV
Pigeon Hawk–CV
Sparrow Hawk–CV

Grouse Family

Blue Grouse–R; Y-S
Sage Grouse–CV

Pheasant Family

California Quail–R; F-Y
Mountain Quail–R; Y-L

Rail Family

Virginia Rail–CV
Sora–CV
American Coot–CV

Plover Family

Killdeer–SV

Sandpiper Family

Common Snipe–C
Spotted Sandpiper–SV
Solitary Sandpiper–CV
Wandering Tattler–CV
Willet–CV
Lesser Yellowlegs–M
Baird's Sandpiper–CV
Least Sandpiper–CV

Stilt Family

American Avocet–CV
Black-necked Stilt–CV

Phalarope Family

Red Phalarope–CV
Wilson's Phalarope–CV
Northern Phalarope–CV

Skua Family

Parasitic Jaeger–CV

Gull-Tern Family

Herring Gull–CV
California Gull–CV
Ring-billed Gull–CV
Bonaparte's Gull–CV

Pigeon Family

Band-tailed Pigeon–SV; F-Y
Mourning Dove–CV

Cuckoo Family

Roadrunner–CV; F

Owl Family

Barn Owl–CV
Screech Owl–R; F-Y
Flammulated Owl–CV
Great Horned Owl–R; F-S
Pygmy Owl–R; Y-L
Spotted Owl–R; Y
Great Gray Owl–R; L
Long-eared Owl–R; F-Y
Short-eared Owl–CV
Saw-whet Owl–R; Y-L

Goatsucker Family

Poorwill–SV; LS-Y
Common Nighthawk–SV; Y-L

Swift Family

Black Swift–SV; Y
Vaux's Swift–CV
White-throated Swift–SV; F-Y

Hummingbird Family

Black-chinned Hummingbird–SV; F-Y
Anna's Hummingbird–R; F-Y
Rufous Hummingbird–M; Y
Allen's Hummingbird–CV
Calliope Hummingbird–CV; Y-L

Kingfisher Family

Belted Kingfisher–R; F-Y

Woodpecker Family

Red-shafted Flicker–R; F-L
Pileated Woodpecker–R; Y-L
Acorn Woodpecker–R; F-Y
Lewis' Woodpecker–R; F-Y
Yellow-bellied Sapsucker–WV or R; Y-L
Williamson's Sapsucker–R;L-S

Woodpecker Family (Cont.)

Hairy Woodpecker–R; F-L
Downy Woodpecker–R; F-Y
Nuttall's Woodpecker–CV; F
White-headed Woodpecker–R; Y-L
Black-backed Three-toed Woodpecker–R; L-S

Tyrant Flycatcher Family

Western Kingbird–CV; F
Kiskadee Flycatcher–CV
Ash-throated Flycatcher–CV; F
Black Phoebe–SV; F
Say's Phoebe–CV; F
Traill's Flycatcher–SV; F-L
Hammond's Flycatcher–SV; L
Dusky Flycatcher–SV; L
Gray Flycatcher–CV
Western Flycatcher–SV; F-Y
Western Wood Pewee–SV; F-S
Olive-sided Flycatcher–SV; Y-L

Lark Family

Horned Lark–CV; F

Swallow Family

Violet-green Swallow–SV; F-Y
Tree Swallow–CV; F-Y
Rough-winged Swallow–CV; F
Barn Swallow–CV
Cliff Swallow–SV; F-Y
Purple Martin–CV

Jay Family

Steller's Jay–R; Y-L
Scrub Jay–R; F
Black-billed Magpie–CV; F-Y
Yellow-billed Magpie–CV; F-Y
Common Raven–CV
Common Crow–CV; F-Y
Piñon Jay–CV; F-Y
Clark's Nutcracker–R; L-S

(Continued)

155

Tit Family

Mountain Chickadee–R; Y-S
Plain Titmouse–R; F
Common Bushtit–R; F

Nuthatch Family

White-breasted Nuthatch–R; F-S
Red-breasted Nuthatch–R; Y-S
Pygmy Nuthatch–R; Y-L

Creeper Family

Brown Creeper–R; Y-L

Wrentit Family

Wrentit–R; F-Y

Dipper Family

Dipper (Water Ouzel)–R; Y-S

Wren Family

House Wren–SV; F-Y
Winter Wren–R & WV; Y-L
Bewick's Wren–R; F
Long-billed Marsh Wren–WV; F-Y
Cañon Wren–R; F-Y
Rock Wren–R & SV; F-S

Thrasher Family

Mockingbird–R; F
California Thrasher–R; F
Sage Thrasher–CV

Thrush Family

Robin–SV; Y-S
Varied Thrush–WV; F-L
Hermit Thrush–SV & WV; Y-S
Swainson's Thrush–SV; F-L
Western Bluebird–WV; F-Y
Mountain Bluebird–SV; Y-S
Townsend's Solitaire–SV or R; Y-S

156

Old World Warbler Family

Blue-gray Gnatcatcher–SV; F
Golden-crowned Kinglet–SV; Y-L
Ruby-crowned Kinglet–R & WV; L

Pipit Family

Water Pipit–WV

Waxwing Family

Bohemian Waxwing–CV
Cedar Waxwing–WV & M

Silky Flycatcher Family

Phainopepla–R; F

Shrike Family

Northern Shrike–CV
Loggerhead Shrike–CV; F

Vireo Family

Hutton's Vireo–R; F-Y
Solitary Vireo–SV; F-L
Warbling Vireo–SV; F-L

Wood Warbler Family

Orange-crowned Warbler–SV; F-L
Nashville Warbler–SV; Y-L
Yellow Warbler–SV; F-Y
Myrtle Warbler–CV
Audubon's Warbler–SV & WV; F-S
Black-throated Gray Warbler–SV;
  F-Y
Townsend's Warbler–CV; Y
Hermit Warbler–SV; Y-L
MacGillivray's Warbler–SV; Y-L
Yellowthroat–CV; F
Yellow-breasted Chat–CV; F-Y
Wilson's Warbler–SV; F-L

Weaver Finch Family

House Sparrow–CV

Blackbird Family

Western Meadowlark–R; F-Y
Yellow-headed Blackbird–CV; F-Y
Redwinged Blackbird–SV; F-Y
Bullock's Oriole–CV
Brewer's Blackbird–SV; F-L
Brown-headed Cowbird–CV; F-Y

Tanager Family

Western Tanager–SV; Y-L

Sparrow Family

Black-headed Grosbeak–SV; F-Y
Blue Grosbeak–CV; F
Lazuli Bunting–SV; F-Y
Evening Grosbeak–SV; Y-L
Purple Finch–CV; F-Y
Cassin's Finch–R; Y-S
House Finch–R; F
Pine Grosbeak–R; L-S
Gray-crowned Rosy Finch–R; S-A
Pine Siskin–R; Y-S
American Goldfinch–CV

Lesser Goldfinch–CV; F-Y
Lawrence's Goldfinch–CV
Red Crossbill–R; L-S
Green-tailed Towhee–SV; Y-S
Rufous-sided Towhee–R; F-Y
Brown Towhee–CV; F-Y
Savannah Sparrow–CV; F-Y
Vesper Sparrow–CV; F-L
Lark Sparrow–CV; F
Rufous-crowned Sparrow–CV; F
Sage Sparrow–CV; F
Slate-colored Junco–CV
Oregon Junco–SV; Y-S
Chipping Sparrow–SV; F-Y
Brewer's Sparrow–CV; F-Y
Harris' Sparrow–CV
White-crowned Sparrow–SV & WV;
   Y-S
Golden-crowned Sparrow–WV;
   F-L
White-throated Sparrow–CV
Fox Sparrow–SV & WV; F-H
Lincoln's Sparrow–SV; L
Song Sparrow–R; F-S

REPTILES AND AMPHIBIANS IN THE PARK

Next lower in the evolutionary scale below the birds and mammals stand the reptiles, including the snakes, turtles, and lizards, and next below them the group known as amphibians comprising the frogs, toads, and salamanders. Yosemite National Park contains twenty-three species in the first-named group and nine in the second. Among all these "cold-blooded" vertebrates there is but one poisonous species, the Pacific Rattlesnake (*Crotalus viridus oreganus*). All the snakes, even the rattler, will slip away quietly unless cornered and provoked into fighting.

As a rule, the numbers of both species and individuals decrease with altitude. Above 6,000 feet there are but few reptiles, though amphibians are well represented as to individuals. One species in the latter group, the Pacific Tree-toad (*Hyla regilla*), may be heard in spring at almost all altitudes. Although scarcely an inch in

157

length, it is notably hardy and ranges up even to timberline. In the high mountain meadows (above 6,500 feet) will be found a toad peculiar to the region, the Yosemite Toad (*Bufo canorus*), and its mellow notes are pleasing additions to the chorus of bird songs just after the snow leaves. The California Toad (*Bufo boreas halophilus*) is a large one commonly found at elevations up to 4,500 feet. California Yellow-legged Frogs (*Rana boylii boylii*) and Sierra Yellow-legged Frogs (*Rana boylii sierrae*) throng all the stream sides and lake margins up to timberline. The California Red-Legged Frog (*Rana aurora draytonii*) is by far the largest of the Park's frogs, but it is not very abundant even in its lower elevation range.

The salamanders are less in evidence, and careful search is required to locate them. The Sierra Newt (*Taricha taricha sierrae*), often commonly called water dog or mud puppy, is probably the most common salamander found in Yosemite National Park, while the Sierra Nevada Salamander (*Ensatina eschaltzi platensis*) is the only spotted member found within the Park's boundaries. The other species, the Mount Lyell Salamander (*Hydromantes platycephalus*), is found only at Yosemite, and only at higher elevations.

The Western Pond Turtle (*Clemmys marmorata*) is the only representative of its family found in the Park; it has not yet been discovered much higher than the 3,000-foot level in the western foothills. Of the nine kinds of lizards the most common and most widely distributed group comprises the "Swifts" (*Sceloporus*) which live about trees and on rocks and logs. These are darkbodied, with more or less blue on the undersurface. The Alligator Lizards (*Gerrhonotus*) which have long slender bodies, small legs and large diamond-shaped heads are found in grass and under brush piles and chaparral. These are reputed to be poisonous, but their only defense when handled is to give their captor a sharp pinch in their relatively heavy jaws. They have no poison glands. In the leafy debris beneath the golden oaks along the walls of the Valley there is the large Yosemite Skink (*Eumeces gilberti*) which has a pinkish-red head and olive-green body. It has exceedingly smooth scales and can slip through one's fingers as if oiled.

The snakes of the region comprise thirteen species. In the Yosemite Valley is found the Pacific Rubber Snake (*Charina bottae*), a smooth scaled "double-ended" relative of the pythons and boas of the tropics, but not known to exceed 30 inches in length. There are three species of Garter Snakes (*Thamnophis*) in the Park. They usually show a preference for moist meadows and the margins

158

of pools and may usually be identified at once by the three light-yellow stripes along the body, one on each side and the third along the middle of the back.

The most beautiful of the local snakes is the Sierra Coral King Snake (*Lampropeltis multicincta*), a small, smooth-scaled, perfectly harmless species that lives along the golden-oak talus slopes and is frequently met with on the lower trails. Its banded coloration is of black, red, and yellow, all of bright tone. Another of Yosemite's small snakes is the Spotted Night Snake (*Hypsiglena ochrorhyncha*). Adults seldom reach a length greater than 15 to 20 inches and are a dullish-white color with innumerable tiny specks of brown to black. Of course, the smallest and rarest is the Sharp-tailed Snake (*Contia tenuis*) which seldom exceeds a length of 12 or 14 inches. It is rather stout for its length, and the tail quickly tapers to a sharp point.

The California King Snake (*Lampropeltis getulus californiae*), so conspicuous because of its pattern of black and white rings, is one of the Park's larger snakes. Another species that is easy to identify is the Coral-bellied Ring-necked Snake (*Diadophis amabilis pulchellus*), for it is the only snake found in Yosemite that has the single light-colored ring around the neck. This small snake has an orange to reddish belly, while the dorsal surface is uniformly dull-olive to bluish-gray colored. The Western Blue Racer (*Coluber constrictor mormon*) and the California Striped Whipsnake (*Coluber lateralis*) are both very long (up to 4½ feet) and slender and capable of moving rapidly. Both prefer the more open brushy hillsides and dry grassy meadows. The western blue racer may be readily distinguished from the whipsnake because the former is uniformly colored a bluish-brown, and without any indication of lateral or dorsal striping, while the latter is dark-brown and with two very distinct lateral light lines that extend the full length of the body. The Pacific Gopher Snake (*Pituophis catenifer*), oftentimes called "bull snake," is not widely distributed in Yosemite National Park, but seems confined to the lower elevations. It is not primarily a snake of the forested and rocky areas but rather of the open grass-lands, sandy foothills, and valleys. The dark ocher-yellow-colored gopher snake is probably the largest snake found in this region, for they are rather bulky in addition to the fact that they sometimes reach a length of 3 to 4 feet.

The Pacific Rattlesnake is likely to be found anywhere in the Yosemite National Park below about 7,000 feet altitude, but in Yosemite Valley, and along the well-traveled trails so many of the

159

snakes have been killed that the species is becoming rare in most of these places. The rattler has many distinctive features, and in consequence will be recognized at once, even by persons who know it only by reputation. The head is bluntly triangular, the neck constricted; the stout body is covered with ridged or keeled scales, and the short tail has at the end a short segmented rattle which the animal can vibrate to produce the well-known warning sound.

FISH OF THE PARK

The original fish fauna of Yosemite National Park is not a rich one. Of native species there are one Sucker, three Minnows, one Sculpin, and one Trout; and of these only the trout was at all common. But, today four species of trout are planted in the waters of the Park to provide sport and recreation for the visitor while he is enjoying the beauty of the region. The following is a description of the various sporting fish which may be found in the Park.

RAINBOW TROUT (*Salmo gairdneri irideus*)

This is the only species of trout native to the waters of Yosemite National Park, all other kinds having been introduced. Its body is usually profusely spotted with dark spots on lighter background; a rosy lateral band extends along the sides; no red or brown spots on the sides; the back often bluish-gray; abdomen silvery-white. Extensively propagated artificially and planted in many lakes and streams throughout the Park. An 18- to 20-inch fish may weigh from 2 to 4 pounds. Average size for two- or three-year-old fish is about 10 inches. A spring spawner.

CUTTHROAT TROUT (*Salmo clarki*)

This trout can be distinguished from the rainbow trout—the species it most nearly resembles—by the presence of red dash-marks on the membranes of the lower jaw (hence the name), by the presence of teeth at the base of the tongue (on the hyoid bone), and by the lack of the red stripe on the sides. At present, the cutthroat is considered of minor importance in Yosemite National Park. A spring spawner.

160

GOLDEN TROUT (*Salmo agua bonita*)

The top of its head, back, upper parts of its sides are yellowish-olive; a bright carmine stripe extends along its sides; lower sides are bright golden-yellow fading into a greenish-white below orange-yellow belly; sides of its head are rosy; ten or so parr marks on its sides; dorsal fin tipped with orange; ventrals and anal tipped in white. Spring spawner.

BROOK TROUT (*Salvelinus fontinalis*)

An introduced species planted extensively in many Park waters, particularly at the higher altitudes. This charr spawns from October to December. The marbled pattern of light spots on darker background, red spots on sides, and lower reddish fins tipped broadly with white, serve to distinguish this charr from the trout. The head, back, dorsal, and caudal fins are spotted with dark-olive or black. Under sides are reddish sometimes brilliant; ventral surface tinged with pink. Parr marks are found on large fish. Red spots on sides surrounded with light greenish-brown.

BROWN TROUT (*Salmo trutta*)

This trout is valued because it is a fall spawner, and because it withstands heavy angling pressure better than other species. The backs and sides are brown, olive-brown, greenish or grayish; lighter on the sides; and silvery or white beneath. The back is covered with dark, almost black spots; sides have red spots encircled with light rings. Attains length of 25 inches and 6 pounds in weight. It is a voracious fish, not easily caught always, and less likely to be fished out. An exotic which is not propagated artificially in the Park.

This is the complete listing of sporting fish found in the Park. Some fishermen try to catch the Sacramento Sucker which is rather abundant in the lower Merced and Tuolumne river systems. This sucker may be distinguished from all other fishes of Yosemite by its yellow-brown coloration and the disc-like protuberance of the flattened upper lip.

The Sacramento Squawfish, a member of the minnow family, is occasionally caught by fishermen in the waters about El Portal and in the pools of the Merced canyon. It furnishes good sport, fighting

161

vigorously for a short time after being hooked. The squawfish can be distinguished by its large head, large mouth, the lack of jaw teeth and adipose fin, and the elongated, pike-like body which is muddy-green all over, except for silver on the sides. The two other minnow species found in the Park—the California Roach and the Hardhead—and the Riffle Sculpin are rarely caught by fishermen.

INSECTS IN THE PARK

Insects are part of the Park's wildlife. Of course, to many visitors the word "insect" conjures up all kinds of creepy crawly "bugs"— yet to those who are at all interested in Nature, the study of entomology is a most fascinating one. The insect fauna of Yosemite National Park is especially rich. Indeed, so numerous are the species that many will be noticed by even the most casual observer. But, in this book, it would be impossible to mention all the species. If you are interested in identifying those multi-colored butterflies or day-flying moths that are seen about the Park, it would be wise to purchase one of the books on the subject from the Yosemite Natural History Association (see page 203).

Chapter 7.

Things to Do in the Park

WHILE sightseeing is the major activity of visitors to Yosemite National Park, there are many other things to do. You may wish to fish . . . swim . . . or even go bicycling. In winter you can ski, skate, toboggan, or sleigh ride. Let us look in detail at some of the activities available in the Park.

FISHING IN THE PARK

Where to fish is the question foremost in your mind when you come into a new place to try your luck. Here in Yosemite National Park, trout have been planted in over 200 lakes and in 550 miles of streams from one end of the Park to the other. These waters are kept stocked either by natural or artificial means. As a general rule, the best angling is found in the waters far from the areas where visitors usually congregate. (Actually, only Tenaya Lake and Hetch Hetchy Reservoir, of the better fishing spots, can be reached by car. All others require back-country travel.) But, since trout populations often fluctuate radically and conditions of Park waters vary from year to year, check at the Ranger Station nearest the area that you wish to fish for the best spots. You can then purchase a topographical map of Yosemite National Park (see page 204). This map will serve as a trail guide and, also, will show the location of the lakes and streams that the Ranger suggests.

When to fish? The open season for fishing and the daily and possession limit for the species of fish found in the Park conform with regulations of the State of California for the Central Sierra Region. A cooperative arrangement exists between the National

163

Park Service and the California Department of Fish and Game whereby fish for planting purposes are provided by the state. In turn, a California angling license, plus two license stamps, is required for all persons over 16 years of age fishing within the Park. State angling licenses and stamps may be obtained at the general stores in Yosemite Valley, Wawona, Tuolumne Meadows, and at the High Sierra Camps.

While a few of the streams which can be reached during the early portion of the season do sometimes produce fair catches for the skilled angler or bait fisherman, the best results are usually obtained around July 1 when the water becomes clear after the spring runoff. For the remainder of the summer, most of the streams are good for fly and lure fishing. But, in the fall, when the streams are low, only the skilled fisherman can hope for any success at all.

Lake fishing is generally at its best during the first few weeks after the ice leaves the lake. (For most lakes located below 10,000 feet this usually occurs by July 15.) Then, during August, fishing success becomes rather uncertain due to several factors. First of all, the fish seek the cooler waters in the depth of the lakes as the surface temperatures warm up. Also during this period, more food is available and the anglers' offerings are less attractive. But, some of the best *lake* fishing can be had in September and October when cooler temperatures change these conditions.

Trout feed actively for brief periods each day or night. Although these times may vary, as a rule, the best fishing is to be had in early morning and evening. A midday lull is sometimes experienced on large lakes. In addition, afternoon winds often create a heavy rippling on the surface which reduces angling success. Smaller lakes and streams are influenced less by these feeding periods and may be good fishing all day.

The use of boats, rafts, canoes, or other floating craft are only permitted on Tenaya Lake, Merced Lake, May Lake, Benson Lake, Tilden Lake, Many Island Lake, Twin Lakes, and Kibbie Lake. The use of any type of motor on them is prohibited. While no boats, canoes, or rafts are permitted on the waters of Yosemite Valley, swimming aids such as life preservers, inner tubes, and air mattresses are allowed on the Merced River from the upper end of Camp 11 to a point 200 feet upstream from the diversion dam at the intersection of the Big Oak Flat Road (Route 120) and the All-year Highway (Route 140). Complete fishing regulations may be obtained at the various District Ranger Stations (see page 80).

164

Many of the high country lakes, such as Rodgers Lake, offer fine fishing. National Park Service photo

WINTER IN THE PARK

Winter is very special in Yosemite National Park. The far Sierra peaks are coated in white, and the snows have spilled down, crusting the pines and oaks of the great Valley. It is splendidly quiet. The waterfalls now are but wisps that splash into the still river. And an occasional squirrel patters across a snow-carpeted meadow. Winter is a special time to enjoy the Park: from the grandeur of the Valley to the excitement of winter sports and skiing up on the slopes at Badger Pass.

By mid-December there is usually sufficient snow for good skiing and this condition continues through April. Actually, the Valley, in a normal year, receives about 90 inches of snowfall throughout the winter months, with long stretches of clear, bright weather in between the snowstorms. Of course, at the higher altitudes in the Park, the snowfall is greater and the snow piles to greater depths. The Badger Pass winter sports area, at an elevation of 7,300 feet, enjoys ideal ski conditions.

The Arch Rock Entrance on the Merced Road (State Route 140), the South Entrance (State Route 41) and the Big Oak Flat Entrance (State Route 120 from the west) remain open the year around. While they may not be required during your winter visit, bring tire chains with you, for you are liable to awaken some morning to a fall of fresh snow of several inches.

The Awahnee and the Yosemite Lodge are open throughout the year. Camp Curry opens for the winter season in later December and remains open during the height of the skiing season. Reservations should be made for holidays and weekends. For those hardy souls who like winter camping, Camp 4, in the warmest part of the Valley, is kept open except during brief periods when the snow is so deep that camping is impossible. House trailers may also use Camp 4. The general store and many other facilities are open during the winter to serve the permanent population of National Park Service and the Yosemite Park and Curry Co. employees.

In the Valley at midday, the mercury will stand around 45 degrees or higher, while at night it will drop to 25 degrees or lower. But freezing nights in Yosemite Valley result in excellent skating on the large outdoor rink at Camp Curry. Skate rental is available.

The Badger Pass winter sports area, 6 miles from Chinquapin Junction on the Glacier Point Road, and 21 miles from Yosemite Valley, is the center of skiing activity. (For those without autos, bus service from Yosemite Valley to Badger Pass is available dur-

In winter a spectacular cone of ice forms at the base of Upper Yosemite Fall. Ice frozen on the face of the cliff thunders down when loosened by the morning sun. National Park Service photo

ing the winter season.) Here, the skiing is very comfortable—family-style, nothing too pretentious about it. There are several challenging runs for the experts, but mostly Badger is a panorama of pleasant slopes just for the fun of skiing—and for the fun of learning. Whether you are five or fifty, Badger is a good place to start. When the bell rings for ski class, there is plenty of company, and a staff of understanding instructors. Once you have the feel of the runs, you will find it fun to compete for a club pin or try out on the Flying Fifty course. Several times during the week and on Sunday afternoons, the Yosemite Winter Club schedules competitions: Slaloms, proficiency tests, Flying Fifty races and "Y" tests. Lots of champions have left their names and first records burned into the skis that line the wall of the ski house.

Right at the foot of the slopes, you will find the Badger ski house—never too far away for a brief rest, a fast lunch at the cafeteria or snack bar—or to enjoy some of the camaraderie of ski-talk. Or lunch can be a real occasion in the Snowflake Room atop the ski house. Help yourself to the grand buffet, warm the cockles of your heart with a decanter of wine, and relax. On a sunny day you will pick up a nice winter tan on the broad outside deck—all the while watching the action and color of the Badger slopes. Children are probably building a snowman off to one side, while another small slope has been taken over for snow-platter racing. The ski house at Badger has all the services you will want—rental and ski shop; first-aid room, plus the Ski Tots Playhouse for children. An attendant keeps an eye on the children and can arrange for naps and a bit of quiet play.

The following is a description of lift facilities at Badger Pass:

Installation	Length	Vertical Rise	Capacity/Hour
Lift (Chair) Riblet	3,500 feet	566 feet	1,000
#1 Lift (T-Bar) Constam	3,300 feet	550 feet	1,000
#2 Lift (T-Bar) Constam	1,800 feet	365 feet	900
#3 Lift (T-Bar) Constam	865 feet	260 feet	900
#4 Lift (T-Bar) Hall	1,600 feet	315 feet	1,000

Ski touring in Yosemite National Park is a popular winter pastime. Here skier leaves Badger Pass Ski House. National Park Service photo

While at Badger, you may wish to take the snomobile sightseeing trip. This motorized sleigh takes you over the top of the ski area for a rare winter view of some of the famed Yosemite country under winter conditions. Bring a camera along—the sight of Cloud's Rest or the Cathedral Range is exceptional and spectacular. Chances are good that you will spot some wildlife, too.

Adventurous skiers may want to enjoy some of the Yosemite winter beauty to be found by touring. You may join a short, easy picnic tour—or plan an overnight stay. Ski-touring parties are arranged to Ostrander Lake Hut; or to Glacier Point Mountain House with its breath-taking view. *Warning:* Touring skiers should keep on the signed ski trails and avoid undertaking too strenuous trips. Do not start on any ski run later than 4 P.M., as darkness comes early. Avoid lengthy trips afield without an experienced leader. Before undertaking any ski-tour journey, consult with the ranger on duty at Badger Pass.

Evenings are a good time in Yosemite Valley. Accommodations are here (see page 166), and there is always plenty to do. At the Ahwahnee there are frequent ski supper dances. Or you may wish to take a twirl on the outdoor ice rink at Camp Curry—or join a group for a pleasant evening around the fire. Films and Park Naturalist programs are part of the Yosemite winter schedule as well.

The Bracebridge Dinner. One of the outstanding traditional winter events in Yosemite is the Bracebridge Dinner. It is presented twice each Christmas night, December 25, at 5 P.M. and at 8:45 P.M. in the dining room of the Ahwahnee. It has been held annually since 1927, save for the years of World War II, when the Ahwahnee served as a U.S. Navy Hospital.

The costuming of the participants, the music, both the selection and presentation, the book, the magnificence of the decorated dining room and, finally, the splendid dinner itself all blend to create a mood and atmosphere dramatic and moving. Based loosely on Washington Irving's *Sketch Book* account of a typical Yorkshire Christmas dinner in the manor of Squire Bracebridge during the reign of George III, The Ahwahnee's pageant contains subtleties of costume, food, music, and mummery that lift it gently from that highly traditional affair. Reservations in advance.

OTHER ACTIVITIES IN THE PARK

In addition to fishing and the winter sports discussed in this chapter, and hiking and riding covered in Chapter 4, there are many other activities available to the Park visitor.

Swimming. Public heated swimming pools are located at Yosemite Lodge and at Camp Curry—open during the summer season. There is a general admission fee; however, no charge for guests of the Lodge or Camp. During the months of July and August water temperatures (while cool) in the Merced River are suitable for swimming, and miles of sandy beaches are available on the floor of Yosemite Valley for sun-bathing. (There are *no* lifeguards along the Merced River and any swimming that is done here is at your own risk.) There is a heated pool at The Ahwahnee for hotel guests.

Bicycling. Bicycles are available for rental during the spring, summer, and fall season at Camp Curry, Yosemite Lodge, Camp 14, and the Housekeeping Camp. The level Valley floor with its many miles of roads is ideal for cycling.

Dancing. There is dancing nightly except Sunday throughout the year in The Indian Room at The Ahwahnee. No cover charge. Cocktail service is available.

Golf. A public nine-hole championship length course (3,035 yards —par 35) is located at Wawona. There is an experienced professional in charge of the course. Clubs may be rented. A nine-hole pitch-and-putt course is located on the grounds of The Ahwahnee. Clubs may be rented.

Tennis. Hard-surfaced tennis courts are located on the grounds of The Ahwahnee and at Wawona. No charge to hotel guests.

Films and outdoor programs are held nightly at Camp Curry and Yosemite Lodge during the summer months.

OTHER THINGS TO SEE IN THE PARK

In Chapter 2, there was a full discussion on the things to see by auto in the Park, while many of the natural points of interest that only may be seen by foot or from a saddle were described in Chapter 3. Here are some of the man-made features that you should take in while in Yosemite National Park.

THE NATURALIST PROGRAM

From the Visitor Center at Park Heaquarters in Yosemite Village, there is conducted a lively summer program of naturalist activities for every age and interest, from armchair travel to mountain climbing. Even if you are in the Park for only a limited time, by all means make at least one visit to the Visitor Center, and take part in its programs if you can.

While in the Visitor Center area, take time for a stroll through the cool, sweet-smelling wild-flower garden. Here twice a day in the Indian Circle, a naturalist shows how the Indians lived, hunted, cooked, and dressed. There are also Indian basketry demonstrations held here during the weekdays.

Across the street and to the west of the Yosemite Visitor Center is the Pioneer Cemetery, the final resting place of several people who played important parts in the growth and development of Yosemite National Park. The cemetery was laid out during the last century, perhaps the 1870's. At that time Yosemite Valley was under the guardianship of the State of California. Early pioneers had been buried in various places in the valley. Later the graves that were known were moved to this location. In 1906 the cedar trees were planted, and the fence that surrounds the cemetery was put in place. Perhaps you would care to take a few minutes to gaze back into Yosemite's interesting past by wandering through this fascinating place.

While in Yosemite Valley, be sure to visit the Happy Isles Nature Center at its upper end. Exhibits here stress back-country travel and wild animals plus a short slide program of back-country enjoyment.

Pioneer Yosemite History Center. For those interested in history, a stop at the Pioneer History Center and its famous covered bridge is a must. From 1857, this covered bridge has spanned the South Fork of the Merced River at Wawona. From the time when Galen Clark built it, it existed as a simple, open structure until 1875 when the Washburn brothers rebuilt it as a covered bridge reminiscent of their native Vermont. It carried all traffic—foot, horse, stage, and car—until 1931 when a modern concrete bridge on the new Wawona road replaced it. After its back was broken by the damaging floods of 1955, the covered bridge was restored authentically and painstakingly, even to using square nails, by the National Park Service.

It stands now as the only covered bridge left in any National

172

Junior Rangers on a field trip with Park Naturalists. National Park Service photo

Park and one of the few in the West. It is used daily by horses and visitors as the central feature of the Pioneer Yosemite History Center. On the south side of the river in the old wagon shop are historical exhibits showing the transportation used by early pioneers. On the north side is a collection of authentic, historic buildings, furnished to show the type of housing the pioneers had—including the fieldstone jail.

The Pioneer Center which opened officially in 1961, attracts many visitors who appreciate its unique historical values. It is significant that these old buildings are gathered together at Wawona, where the first pioneer activity of any magnitude took place in the early 1850's. Exhibits, self-guiding pamphlets, and tape

173

recordings in each building assure visitors of sharing the history of Yosemite and its human builders.

The old Wawona Hotel (see page 184) looks down from a rise above the History Center. It is one of the few early resort hotels left in the west today. It was in its heyday when the stagedriver was King of the Road. The hotel was midway between the end of the railroad at Raymond and Yosemite Valley—a day's ride from each.

Other Naturalist Outposts. There are other branch-museums and naturalist service at several focal points of interest. At Mariposa Grove the old log cabin originally built by Galen Clark and replaced by the State in 1885 has been reconstructed. This is now equipped as a museum telling the complete story of the Big Trees. A Park Naturalist is stationed here to lecture, make guide trips, and give accurate information.

The Glacier Point Lookout is located on the most famed scenic point on the rim. Powerful binoculars enable visitors to bring the Sierra's great peaks to their very feet.

Walks and Hikes. There are easy, guided nature walks each summer morning through the Valley and at Wawona, Glacier Point, Bridalveil Campground, White Wolf Campground, Mariposa Grove, and Tuolumne Meadows. More vigorous all-day hikes leave twice weekly from the Valley and almost daily from Tuolumne Meadows. Schedules for all Park Naturalist conducted activities are posted on bulletin boards at various locations in the Park, or inquire at the Visitor Center information counter.

Campfire Programs (summer only). Informal outdoor programs are held nightly except Sunday in Yosemite Valley as noted on the Visitor Center bulletin board; and at Glacier Point, Wawona, Bridalveil Creek Campground, Tenaya Lake, White Wolf Campground, Crane Flat Campground, and Tuolumne Meadows several nights a week. At these programs, Park Naturalists tell the story of Yosemite in its various aspects. There are also illustrated talks given at The Ahwahnee, Camp Curry, Yosemite Lodge, Wawona Hotel, and the Big Trees Lodge several nights a week.

Junior and Senior Rangers (summer only). Students in Grades 3 through 9 and above are invited to become junior and senior rangers at a program given mornings from Monday through Friday.

They will learn about animals, trees, and wildflowers, and will make a nature notebook. Campfire programs, with such themes as Indians or the rocks of Yosemite, are held each week. *Senior Ranger* (students in Grades 7, 8, 9, or above) *patches* featuring Yosemite Falls and *Junior Ranger patches* with Half Dome are awarded to students who are present five days and complete all work. But each student gets a certificate of completion for the number of days attended. Schedules and meeting places are posted on bulletin boards.

THE FIREFALL

The Firefall has been traditional in Yosemite National Park for more than sixty years. The millions of visitors who have witnessed this unique and thrilling spectacle cherish it among their most vivid and colorful memories of the Park. Each evening during the summer season the stream of glowing embers pours from the edge of Glacier Point, 3,254 feet above Camp Curry. This sight of unsurpassed beauty is visible from most open areas in the eastern end of the Valley. Sometimes the embers pour straight down the cliff, gradually spreading fanwise as they approach the ledge below; again the stream of fire waves back and forth in its descent in the manner of a windblown waterfall. It continues for several minutes, and as the last mass of embers is pushed over the cliff a shower of sparks and flame arise momentarily. Thereafter the glow fades very gradually and dies away, leaving the cliff to darkness and many a watcher close to tears.

A considerable measure of skill is required in the preparation and execution of an effective Firefall. Therefore, the responsibility is vested in one employee who prepares the bonfire in the morning, lights it as seven o'clock in the evening, and pushes it over the cliff at nine. The fuel consist entirely of bark from fallen red fir trees which is gathered in an area near Glacier Point. The fragments of bark are quite small and the fire consumes about half a cord daily. The pile is circular and stands some three feet high when lighted. In the course of two hours it burns down to a mass of incandescent embers about the size of walnuts. When the signal is given from Camp Curry, the "Firefall Man" begins to shove the coals over the cliff with a long-handled iron pusher.

The question of fire hazard is often in the minds of those who watch the stream of burning coals cascade down the cliff. There is no danger as the embers alight upon a wide ledge a thousand feet

175

below the Point. Curiously enough a tall ⁻ed fir tree stands upon this ledge and wildflowers grow out of the ashes of countless Firefalls.

During the long period since its inception, the Firefall has become associated with a traditional procedure which adds greatly to its impressiveness. A few moments before Firefall time lights are extinguished. In the expectant hush which follows, the call "Hello, Glacier!" booms out into the night. Some seconds later the clear, but far-away answer "Hello, Camp Curry!" descends through the silence. Camp Curry then calls, "Let the fire fall!" Glacier Point answers, "All right!" and promptly thereafter the stream of fire begins its downward course over the cliff.

DEVILS POSTPILE NATIONAL MONUMENT

While this national monument, of course, is not a man-made feature, you should make every effort, if time permits, to visit it while in the region. Located just a short distance southeast of Yosemite National Park, its central feature is an extraordinary formation of symmetrical, gray-brown andesitic columns, some of which, rising more than 60 feet above their base, fit closely together like the pipes of a great organ. Among similar formations found in other parts of the world, the Giant's Causeway in Ireland is perhaps the best known. Near Tuolumne Meadows, there is a similar but small formation called the Little Devils Postpile.

The Devils Postpile is a remnant of an andesitic lava flow that originated in what is now known as Mammoth Pass and extended approximately 6 miles down the canyon of the Middle Fork of the San Joaquin River, to a point just beyond Rainbow Fall. This outpouring took place during the later interglacial periods in the Sierra Nevada—at least 915,000 years ago. The andesite cracked into columns as it cooled.

As the Middle Fork glacier advanced, it found this mass of basalt obstructing its path. Since the glacial ice at its maximum was about 1,000 feet thick, it easily overrode the obstruction, and began its extensive quarrying action on the fractured mass. During the thousands of years that the ice held sway, the bulk of this andesitic flow was removed, with only the more resistant parts left standing. Of these, the largest is the Devils Postpile, which is about 900 feet long and 200 feet high.

One side of the Postpile was quarried away by the glacier, leaving exposed a sheer wall of columns 40 to 60 feet high. Many of

176

The famous Yosemite Firefall—a colorful, glowing, 1,000-foot fall of fire spilling over Glacier Point's cliff 3,254 feet above Camp Curry. Yosemite Park and Curry Co. photo

these columns have broken away from the face of the formation and lie in fragments in the talus slope below. While most of the columns are vertical, some are slanting, some are curved, and some radiate from a common center.

The top of the formation presents an unusual sight. Here the cross section of the 3- to 7-sided columns has been worn smooth by the grinding action of the glacier, and the exposed surface has the appearance of a mosaic or tile inlay. The pattern strikingly illustrates the characteristic shape of the columns, which under ideal conditions of rock composition and cooling would theoretically all be hexagonal. A marked trail leads to where the glacial polish can be seen.

Among the other interesting geologic features of the area is the pumice found in the northern part of the monument. This material, an exceedingly porous volcanic rock so light that it will float in water, was deposited in post-glacial times by volcanoes located east and north of the Postpile. These volcanoes, now extinct, were part of a local volcanic system to which the Mono Craters belong. Several bubbling hot springs, one of which is at Reds Meadow, are other evidence of recent volcanic activity. It is thought that most of their heat comes from contact with gases from molten lavas that are in the process of crystallization.

Two miles down the river trail from the Postpile, the Middle Fork of the San Joaquin at Rainbow Fall makes a sheer drop of 140 feet into a deep-green pool. The dark andesitic cliffs contrast strikingly with the white water, and during the middle of the day many rainbows add to the beauty of the scene. Care should be taken when watching the fall from the edge of the gorge, because pumice and flaky stone make the footing dangerous. A short, steep trail leads to the bottom of the waterfall where willows, alders, western white pines, and mountain hemlocks, as well as numerous flowers and grasses, form an enchanting garden. Cars may be driven within ¾ of a mile of the fall via the road to Reds Meadow.

Devils Postpile National Monument, at an elevation of 7,600 feet above sea level, is reached by a 10½ mile drive on a paved road from U.S. Route 395 west, thence 7½ miles of mountain road via Minaret Summit to the Postpile and Reds Meadow.

During summer, Park Rangers are on duty to help visitors and to give occasional naturalist programs. If you need information or are in any difficulty, see a Park Ranger.

178

The Devils Postpile at Devils Postpile National Monument. National Park Service photo

Camping. Near the park ranger station a free campground, with tables and benches, is maintained from about June 15 to October 15, depending upon the weather.

Accommodations and Services. Outside monument boundaries, about 2 miles from the campground, are Reds Meadow Lodge and store, where gasoline and oil, groceries, meals, cabins, a telephone, mail service, and saddle and pack horses are available.

Fishing is permitted in the monument, but hunting is forbidden. A California angling license is required for persons 16 years of age or over.

Hiking. Devils Postpile is one of the key points on the John Muir Trail (see page 108), which runs between Yosemite and Sequoia National Parks. Lone hikers should inform the Park Ranger or neighbors before leaving camp. No lengthy trip should be made alone into the rugged Sierra.

Chapter 8.

Accommodations and Services in the Park

ACCOMMODATIONS in Yosemite National Park are as varied as the scenery. You can find rich elegance at The Ahwahnee, old-fashioned charm at historic Wawona Hotel, or a striking feeling of modern beauty at Yosemite Lodge. For those who really want to "rough-it" there are High Sierra camps and the housekeeping units. Between these extremes the range of lodging is wide, at prices that seem reasonable, all things considered. Speaking of rates, they have been omitted in this chapter, since they may change during the operating season. But remember the rates of the Park concessioners are subject to National Park Service approval.

HOTELS, LODGES, HOUSEKEEPING UNITS, AND CAMPS

These public accommodations are operated by the Yosemite Park and Curry Co. under contract with the Secretary of the Interior. For reservations and current information apply to this company at Yosemite National Park, California 95389. The public accommodations in the Park are as follows:

The Ahwahnee. This is a hotel in the grand manner, right in the center of Yosemite Valley. Rooms are spacious, and the service very personal. Grounds are truly magnificent, and each bedroom has a fine view. The baronial dining hall is open to the public for all meals, and during the summer, there is an outside terrace as well. Comfortable clothes for daytime wear; something slightly more dressy for evenings. After dinner, there is dancing, or movies in one of the lounges. A pitch-and-putt course on the grounds; tennis courts and swimming pool. Accommodations include the main building, as well as eight cottages on the grounds with two or four bedrooms each with bath. Two have private sitting rooms. Rates are the same as in the hotel. The Ahwahnee is open all year, except for a few weeks in late November and early December. American plan, meals included.

Yosemite Lodge. This lodge is one of the most popular places to stay in the Valley. A main building of contemporary design surrounds an outdoor patio, and holds a large lounge, restaurant, cafeteria, cocktail lounge, gift shop and post office. Accommodations range from hotel-type rooms to tent cabins (some cabins with housekeeping facilities, see Housekeeping Camp). There is a swimming pool; you are within walking distance of the village; and Yosemite Falls provides a spectacular backdrop. During summer evenings, there are musical entertainment and movies on the patio. Open all year. European plan, meals not included.

Camp Curry. This is one of the most informal and favorite spots to stay in the Valley. Accommodations are in cabins, some hotel-type rooms, and tent cabins, all set in a fragrant fir and cedar grove at the base of Glacier Point. During the summer season, there is entertainment every evening in the pleasant outdoor amphitheater, and it is from here that the famous Yosemite Firefall is best watched. Meals are served in a fine, new cafeteria, and at two outdoor snack bars. In the main buildings, there are a post office and barber shop. Playground with attendant for the nursery set, and a heated swimming pool. Open from approximately mid-May to Labor Day and from late December to end of skiing season. European plan, meals not included.

182

BELOW: *Yosemite's famous hotel Ahwahnee.* ABOVE: *Guests playing on the pitch-and-putt golf course.* Yosemite Park and Curry Co. photos

Wawona Hotel. The Wawona has wide verandas, wicker chairs, and a glider to rock back and forth in. A smooth, rolling green lawn stretches down to a swimming pool, and across the way is a golf course bordered with dark pines. The rooms are in several large cottages on the grounds. There is a stable nearby; and also the Wawona Pioneer History Center. The Wawona Hotel is located near the South Entrance (Fresno road, State Route 41) and is open from approximately mid-May to Labor Day. American plan, meals included.

Big Trees Lodge. A delightful small lodge in the middle of the magnificent Mariposa grove of Giant Sequoias. There are only eleven rooms, and it is cozy for a group, or even a family reunion. The bedrooms are all comfortable; there is a lounge with fireplace. Meals are cafeteria style, with a large outside patio terrace for dining. The Lodge is close to the South Entrance to the Park (State Route 41) and is open from about mid-May until early October. American plan, meals included.

Glacier Point Hotel. This accommodation is a chalet-type lodge, perched near the edge of Glacier Point, and commanding spectacular views of the Valley, the Sierra, and Vernal and Nevada Falls. Meals are cafeteria-style, and there is a snack shop open in the summer. Next door to the hotel is the famous Mountain House, oldest of the accommodations in the Park. Both are open from approximately mid-May to Labor Day. European plan, meals not included.

Tuolumne Meadows Lodge. High in the Sierra, and within a few yards of a rushing mountain stream, these accommodations are in tent cabins, with wood-burning stoves. The Lodge is open in the summer only, and the main building is a large tent where you will find good meals served, and a lounge area. It is located just off the Tioga Pass Road, near the East Entrance to the Park. Open from late June until mid-September. European plan, meals not included.

White Wolf Lodge. This lodge at 8,000 feet is open approximately from late June until Labor Day. Located a mile from the Tioga Pass Road, it is a comfortable place to enjoy much of the pleasure of the Sierra high-country. A meadow near the middle fork of the Tuolumne River is the setting. Pack and saddle animals at the stable. Rustic cabins and tents. Limited groceries available and

184

ABOVE: *Hotel Wawona, one of Yosemite's earliest resort hotels.*
BELOW: *Big Trees Lodge in the Mariposa Grove of Big Trees.*
Yosemite Park and Curry Co. photos

modest restaurant service. European plan, meals are not included.

Housekeeping Camp. The main section of Housekeeping Camp is ½ mile west of Camp Curry along the Merced River. Here is a choice of accommodations for those wishing to "camp out" with some conveniences of home. New "Duplex" units provide deluxe tents for up to four persons: concrete floors, comfortable beds, your own fenced-in patio, wood-burning stove, electric lights and appliance outlets, tables, chairs, mirrors, and food storage area. Automatic laundry facilities available. "Annex" sleeping tents available for parties larger than four. Linen, blankets, and utensils not furnished but may be rented. Completely furnished tents also in the Main Section (without electric lights; oil lanterns provided). Stoneman Section adjacent to Camp Curry, offers completely furnished tents with electric lights. Open from late May until Labor Day. Completely furnished housekeeping cabins with or without private bath available all year at Yosemite Lodge.

High Sierra Camps. As described in Chapter 4, these five camps are accessible only by foot and horse trails. Accommodations are in tents. There are four beds in each; ample blankets and linen. A few private tents available. Good meals are served camp-style; hot showers. Camps are operated on a modified American Plan; rates include dinner, breakfast, and lodging. Box lunches provided at additional charge when requested. Open late June until Labor Day.

Reservations for any of these accommodations should be made well in advance (several months, if possible). Please include: date of arrival, number of persons in party, type of accommodations desired, length of stay, and how arriving (bus or private car). If possible give alternate dates or type of accommodations. Deposit amounting to first day's rate required. Reservations may be made through the Yosemite Park and Curry Co., or through your travel agent. Children under 3 are lodged free; and from 3 to 9 are charged half-rates (except at High Sierra Camps).

There are also accommodations outside the Park at El Portal Administrative Site and on private property at Wawona.

Glacier Point Hotel is situated high above the Valley. Yosemite Park and Curry Co. photo

187

PUBLIC CAMPGROUNDS IN THE PARK

Camping in Yosemite National Park may be divided into two categories—automobile camping and back-country camping. A third type of somewhat similar use is picnicking.

Automobile Camping. Automobile camping and campfires are restricted to the designated auto campgrounds where no campfire permits are required. This type of use includes trailers, pick-up campers, and housecars as well as the traditional "tent" camping. Location of auto camp sites are given later in this chapter.

Back-country Camping. Back-country camping is not restricted, nor is the use of self-contained cooking devices such as gasoline or alcohol stoves. Open campfires and charcoal braziers, however, *are* restricted to designated sites and require campfire permits for their use. A campfire permit will not be issued for any other site except with the express permission of the respective District Ranger.

Picnicking. Picnicking is also not restricted. Picnic fires or other methods of cooking, however, are limited to designated auto campgrounds and certain designated picnic areas. Campfire permits are not required for these designated areas. There are five such picnic areas in Yosemite Valley (Cathedral, El Capitan, Yellow Pine, Rocky Point, and Sentinel), one at Tenaya Lake, and one at Wawona. (No fires are permitted at Cascades Picnic Grounds in the Valley.) Valley picnic area fires must be out by midnight. A campfire permit will not be issued for any other site except with the express permission of the respective District Ranger. Location of major picnic sites are given on mileage tables in Chapter 3.

YOSEMITE VALLEY CAMPGROUNDS—
Elevation about 4,000 feet

General Information. 7-day camping limit June 1 to September 15; 30-day limit balance of the year. Camp 4 is open all year except at times from December to March when snow may be too deep for winter camping. Others open from about May 15 to September 15. All of the following Yosemite Valley campgrounds have flush toilets, tap water, *limited* number of tables and benches, garbage collection, spaces for trailers (except no trailers in Campground 15). No individual campsites or stoves, except as noted for Campgrounds 7 and 15.

188

BELOW: *Modern motel-type units at Yosemite Lodge.* ABOVE: *View from the Mountain Room cocktail lounge.* Yosemite Park and Curry Co. photos

Campground 4. ¼ mile west of Yosemite Lodge. Accommodates 175 camps.

Campground 7. Opposite Campground 15, along Merced River north of and near Camp Curry. 150 individual campsites with fireplaces. Evening naturalist talk.

Campground 11. Near Happy Isles above Camp Curry. Accommodates 700 camps.

Campground 12. Near Yosemite Park and Curry Company stables, parallel to and across river from Campground 14. Accommodates 300 camps.

Campground 14. Northeast of Camp Curry. Part of this camp is along Merced River. Accommodates 800 camps. Outdoor naturalist evening programs. Campground store.

Campground 15. Opposite and across from Campground 7, parallelling Merced River, near Camp Curry. Has 212 individual campsites with concrete fireplaces. No trailer accommodations.

BIG OAK FLAT and
TIOGA ROADS CAMPGROUNDS

General Information. 14-day camping limit in June, July, and August; 30-day limit balance of year. They are generally open, depending on snow conditions, between the end of May and July 1, and close in September or October. All of the following have fireplaces, tables, tap water, flush toilets, and garbage collection:

Hodgdon Meadow. Elevation 4,590 feet. 5 miles west of Crane Flat on Big Oak Flat Road. 110 individual camps and 7 group camps.

Crane Flat. Elevation 6,200 feet. Near junction of Big Oak Flat Road and Tioga Road. 175 individual campsites.

White Wolf. Elevation 8,000 feet. About 1¼ miles west of Tioga Road at White Wolf on the Middle Fork of the Tuolumne River, just beyond White Wolf Lodge. 86 camps.

Tenaya Lake. Elevation 7,600 feet. Adjacent to Tioga Road at west end of lake. Walk-in campground with central parking areas 50 to 200 yards from campsites. 50 camps.

Tuolumne Meadows. Elevation 8,600 feet. 600 camps. Store, post office, gas station, and Ranger Station nearby. Accommodates group camping also.

BELOW: *A portion of famous Camp Curry.* ABOVE: *One of the housekeeping units near the Camp.* Yosemite Park and Curry Company photos

The following campgrounds have tables, stream water, pit toilets, and garbage collection:

Carl Inn. Elevation 4,350 feet. Big Oak Flat Road approximately 7 miles west of Crane Flat. 5 camps.

Tamarack Flat. Elevation 6,315 feet. Adjacent Big Oak Flat Road approximately 3 miles east of Tioga Road (turn off at Gin Flat). Road not suitable for house trailers. 50 camps.

Smoky Jack. Elevation 7,200 feet. Adjacent to Tioga Road approximately 10 miles from Crane Flat. 25 camps.

Yosemite Creek. Elevation 7,200 feet. Near Tioga Road and Yosemite Creek. 30 camps.

Harden Lake. Elevation 7,609 feet. About 3 miles from Tioga Road, 1½ miles beyond White Wolf campground. 10 camps.

Porcupine Creek. Elevation 7,775 feet. Adjacent to Tioga Road, 6 miles west of Tenaya Lake. 10 camps.

Porcupine Flat. Elevation 7,775 feet. Near Tioga Road (on opposite side of road from Porcupine Creek Campground) approximately 6 miles from Tenaya Lake. 50 camps.

GLACIER POINT ROAD CAMPGROUNDS

General Information. 14-day camping limit in June, July, and August; 30-day limit balance of year. The following campsites are open about June 15 to October 1 and have tables, tap water, flush toilets, and garbage collection:

Bridalveil Creek. Elevation 7,200 feet. Adjacent to Glacier Point Road 24 miles from Yosemite Valley. Fireplaces. 126 camps.

Glacier Point. Elevation 7,254 feet. 30 miles from Yosemite Valley. 15 camps.

WAWONA ROAD CAMPGROUND

General Information. 14-day camping limit in June, July, and August; 30-day limit balance of year. The following campsite is open from about April 1 to November 15 and has outdoor tables and benches, fireplaces, piped water, pit and flush toilets, and garbage collection:

Wawona. Elevation 4,096 feet. Located one mile west of Wawona Hotel paralleling South Fork of the Merced River. 187 camps.

Vogelsang camp in High Sierra country. Yosemite Park and Curry Co. photo

ORGANIZED GROUP CAMPGROUNDS

All the campgrounds in Yosemite National Park, except the Tenaya Lake Campground, are available to organized groups as well as individuals. Also, there are two campgrounds for use by organized groups only. All campground use is on a first-come, first-served basis and no space can be reserved in advance.

Camp 9. This camp in Yosemite Valley is limited to organized *youth* groups only, such as Boy Scouts, Girl Scouts, 4-H Clubs, etc. The group may not exceed a total of 75 people. Adult groups and mixed family groups, even though sponsored by a recognized youth group, may not use this campground. Also, house trailers, house cars, and pick-up camper units are not permitted in this camp. Upon arrival in Yosemite Valley, proceed directly to Park Headquarters and register your party with the Ranger on duty. Length of stay is limited to 7 nights during June, July and August—14 nights during the rest of the year.

Tuolumne Meadows Organizational Camp. This facility is available to *any* organized group of not more than 150 people. Upon arrival at Tuolumne Meadows, contact the Ranger on duty at the information station at the campground entrance. He will direct you to the organizational camping area. Length of stay is limited to 14 nights in any calendar year.

There are also group campsites available at Hodgdon Meadow.

CAMPGROUND REGULATIONS

The following are campground regulations that all campers, whether group or individual, must follow:

1. The use of all *public* campgrounds in the Park is on a first-come, first-served basis, even the organized group camping. In most cases, campers should arrive early in the day, preferably *before noon.* No fee is charged for use of campgrounds; reservations are not made. Remember that campgrounds in Yosemite Valley are hotter and more crowded in the summer months than those in outlying districts. Check specific camping regulations on the bulletin board at campground entrance.

2. Campers must register. Locate nearest section-marker post to your campsite, return and fill in all columns of the register. Registration makes it possible for Park Rangers to deliver emergency messages if needed. Emergency messages will be forwarded

by National Park Service personnel only in the event of death or serious illness. Other messages should be directed through the post office or Western Union (see page 197).

3. Keep camp equipment, table, and fire within campground boundary.

4. Do not drive nails into trees or put wire around them.

5. Pets must be on leash, crated, or under *physical* restraint at all times. They must never be allowed to run loose. Pets may be kept overnight in Camp 4 in Yosemite Valley, in the east end of Wawona (Section A), White Wolf (Section C), Bridalveil Creek (Section A) and Yosemite Creek campgrounds; west end of Tuolumne Meadows campground, and Section A of Crane Flat campground. For reasons of sanitation they are *not* permitted in any other campground areas, on beaches, in stores or other public buildings, eating places, or areas where groups of people customarily gather. Pets may be transported or led on leash over or along any road open to public use, but they are not permitted on or along any bridle path or foot trail. Stray dogs and cats running at large may be impounded. In this event, the animal will be placed in the Yosemite Park and Curry Co. kennels in the Yosemite Valley. The owner may claim his pet by payment of kennel fees. In the event the animal is not claimed it will be kept no more than seven days.

6. Use only dead, fallen wood—cut nothing green. (Never gather wood—even dead and fallen—in the Sequoia groves.) Firewood may be purchased at the Housekeeping Camp in Yosemite Valley.

7. Be especially careful with fire. Put out your fire when leaving your campsite.

8. Washbowls are provided in rest rooms. Do not wash at water hydrants or in streams.

9. Please burn cartons and papers. Place wet garbage in trash cans. Leave your camp area clean.

10. In consideration of other campers—quiet between 10 P.M. and 6 A.M. Quiet can be restored if noisy parties are reported immediately to the Ranger Office.

11. One table to a campsite when available.

12. House trailers may park in any of the campgrounds *except* Camp 9 and 15 in Yosemite Valley, and sections of new campground developments at Wawona not designed for trailers. Yosemite Valley, Wawona, Tuolumne Meadows, Crane Flat, Bridalveil and White Wolf camps are equipped with water hydrants,

sanitary facilities, and a limited number of camp tables. There are *no* connections for utilities such as water, sewage, or electricity.

13. Campers desiring to curtain or screen campsites, please select an interior campsite.

14. For sanitary reasons a receptacle must be provided for all sink drainage from trailers. No pits.

15. A good camper will not rake up pine needles or in any way disturb the ground cover.

16. House trailers are not permitted at times during the winter months due to icy or snowy roads. Cars pulling house trailers should enter the Valley via State Route No. 41 from Fresno, State Route No. 140 from Merced, or Big Oak Flat Road (State No. 120). Since portions of State Route No. 120 outside the Park between Tioga Pass Entrance Station and Lee Vining (13.4 miles) are steep and winding, drivers are warned that travel by house trailers may be difficult.

17. Campers shall not leave their camps unattended for more than 48 hours.

18. Only L.P. gas (butane, etc.) equipment meeting Government regulations will be permitted.

19. Deadly fumes or the lack of oxygen have caused fatalities or near fatalities in house trailers and pickup camper units utilizing stoves, heaters, and bottled gas refrigerators which have not been properly vented to the outside. Users of trailers and camper units should be certain that any stoves, heaters, and gas refrigerators are safely vented and that they leave windows *open* when persons are sleeping in each trailer or camper unit.

20. Campfire permits, when required, are not issued for an entire season. They are issued only for a designated area and for a specified time. If there is anything unusual or special (i.e. a group of 30 or more, a group with a large number of stock, persons who appear incapable of making the trip, etc.) about the persons requesting the permit, they should be referred to the District Ranger. Campfire permits must be carried by the party and shown upon request to any Park Ranger or Fire Control Aid. The visitor should be asked to read the instructions on the back of the permit since he agrees to abide by them when he signs the permit. The visitor should be asked to return the permit to the nearest ranger after completing his trip or to mail it to the Superintendant (see page 11 for address).

SERVICES IN THE PARK

Almost every possible tourist service is available to visitors of the Park. They are as follows:

Religious Services. Weekly services for most denominations are held in summer; notices specifying the time and place of each service are posted on bulletin boards at all accommodations, campgrounds, and in other public places. In winter, both Protestant and Roman Catholic services are at the community chapel, which dates from 1879, in the Old Village of Yosemite Valley.

Medical Service. Doctors, nurses, and a dentist are on duty all year at the Lewis Memorial Hospital in Yosemite Village. First aid is available at Ranger Stations. A first-aid station is also maintained in winter at Badger Pass ski house.

Mails Service. The main post office is in the Valley and is open throughout the year, as are offices at Wawona and Yosemite Lodge. Additional summer post offices are located at Camp Curry and Tuolumne Meadows. Letters addressed c/o General Delivery will arrive at the main post office unless addressed to one of the specific post offices; or they can be addressed to you at the lodging unit in which you are staying—for example, Glacier Point Hotel, Yosemite National Park, California 95389. Incidentally, 95389 is the zip code for all the mail stations and addresses in the Park.

Telephone and Telegraph Service. Long-distance calls may be made from public telephones at many locations throughout the Park (Wawona, Glacier Point, White Wolf, Tuolumne Meadows, and several places in the Valley). Western Union telegraph service is available all year at Yosemite Lodge.

Garages, Service Stations. There is a well-equipped garage and repair service in Yosemite Village. Gasoline service stations are located at Camp Curry, the Village, and Yosemite Lodge* Outside the Valley, there are stations at Wawona, Chinquapin Junction* Crane Flat, and Tuolumne Meadows. All stations are Chevron. (*Note:* * Service station open year-round.)

The California State Automobile Association (an affiliate of A. A. A.) maintains a representative in the lobby of the Administration Building at Yosemite Village throughout the summer. There is no N. A. C. representative in Yosemite, but the service garage honors calls from N. A. C. members.

Stores. The Village Store, in Yosemite Village, is open year-round and carries a full line of foodstuffs (including fresh and frozen meats, fruits, and vegetables), drug supplies, clothing, sporting goods, reading materials, curios, souvenirs, and photographic supplies. Small grocery stores are also located at Campground 14 and the concessioner's Housekeeping Camp in summer; at White Wolf —limited supply of staple groceries, about June 15 to September 1; at Wawona Store—limited supply of staple groceries all year; and at Tuolumne Meadows—limited staple groceries, about June 15 to September 15. The Nawassa Shop at Camp Curry has a wide selection of summer clothing.

Photographs and Photo Supplies. Best's Studio, in the Village, specializes in photographic supplies as well as having an excellent selection of gifts, books, and souvenirs. This studio is open all year. The Yosemite Park and Curry Co. has good studios at The Ahwahnee Hotel and Yosemite Lodge, open all year; at Camp Curry, Yosemite Village, Glacier Point, Wawona, and Mariposa Grove during the summer. These studios will accept film for processing.

Gift Shop. Gift shops, in all the major accommodations and in the Village, have a complete supply of curios, souvenirs, newspapers, magazines, books, post cards, and gift items. Some sell limited drug items.

Equipment Rental. Camping supplies, tents, cots, blankets, and cooking utensils may be rented in summer at Housekeeping Camp headquarters; a deposit is required. In Winter, skates and sleds may be rented at Camp Curry, and ski clothing and equipment at Badger Pass.

Laundry. The Yosemite Park and Curry Co. offers fine laundry and dry-cleaning service at the Village Store in the Valley, at Tuolumne Meadows, and at Wawona. There is a self-service laundromat at the Housekeeping Camp in Yosemite Valley in summer. The Village Store also handles shoe repair.

Ice. Ice is available at several locations in Yosemite Valley and at the Wawona Store.

Showers. For a reasonable charge, campers may use the concessioner showers at Yosemite Lodge, Camp Curry, Wawona, Housekeeping Camp, and Tuolumne Meadows.

Dining Service. Meals can be obtained at the Village Restaurant and Coffee Shop, or Degnan's in the Village; at Camp Curry Pavilion Cafeteria and Snack Bars, The Ahwahnee, or Yosemite Lodge (cafeteria or restaurant); at Wawona Hotel, Big Trees Lodge, Glacier Point Hotel, White Wolf Lodge, or Tuolumne Meadows Lodge. Should you choose to picnic, and there are scores of fine spots for this, any of the cafeterias or restaurants will prepare a lunch for you.

Special Meals. There are two special meals available: The Firefall Barbecue and the Horseback Breakfast Ride. The rides are held Monday, Wednesday, and Friday mornings during the summer. Parties ride from stable at 8 A.M. to the breakfasting place on Merced River bank, about an hour's ride. The western-style breakfast includes fresh fruit, eggs, bacon, hot cakes, etc. Cowboy entertainment, ride back to stable.

During the summer season barbecues are held frequently on The Ahwahnee's beautiful grounds. The hearty western meal—charcoal broiled steaks, salad, vegetable, dessert, etc., is followed by campfire singing, lead by cowboy guitarist. Barbecue location allows perfect view of the Firefall from Glacier Point. Please make reservations with your hotel or lodge front desk.

Cocktail and Bar Services. This service is available at The Ahwahnee, Yosemite Lodge, Village Restaurant, Wawona Hotel, and the Wawona Golf Shop Bar.

Barber Shops and Beauty Parlor. Barber shops are located at Camp Curry and Yosemite Village, while there is only a beauty parlor in the Village.

Child Care. For children from one to six years of age, inclusive, the Kiddie Kamp—a completely equipped playground under the supervision of a trained attendant—is maintained at Camp Curry during the summer season. Children 7 to 13, inclusive, may join the Grizzly Club at Camp Curry—games, crafts, hikes, etc. There are also daily burro picnic trips (for 7-to-12-year olds under 110 pounds) and junior riding lessions (for 6 to 13 years). In addition, the National Park Service offers a Junior-Senior Ranger Program which is excellent for youngsters spending a few days in the Park (see page 174-175). Baby-sitting can be arranged at Camp Curry, Yosemite Lodge, Wawona Hotel, and The Ahwahnee.

Pet Care. As previously stated (see page 195), cats and dogs are *not* permitted into any public building in the Park and this, of course, includes hotels, lodges, and camps. The Yosemite Park and Curry Co. maintains fine kennels near the stable in Yosemite Valley and Tuolumne Meadows. These kennels have an experienced attendant in charge.

Pack and Saddle Animals. In summer, experienced riders may rent saddle horses for riding without a guide on the floor of Yosemite Valley; guide service is required elsewhere. Guided saddle trips are scheduled daily both in and out of Yosemite Valley (see Chapter 4 for more details). Saddle animals are available also in summer at Mather, White Wolf Lodge, Tuolumne Meadows Lodge, and Wawona.

Transportation. Motor coach tours can be taken throughout the Valley and to most of the outlying areas (see page 72). Taxi service is available in the Valley itself. Scheduled bus transportation to the Park is available from Merced, Fresno, and Lake Tahoe (see page 14).

Entertainment. See bulletin boards in the hotels, lodges, and camps for daily entertainment schedules. Other activities in the Park are detailed in previous chapter of this book.

SPECIAL NOTICE TO PARENTS

Each year the matter of lost children creates untold anxieties. Throughout the summer there is not a single day in which the Park administration does not receive 5 to 10 lost-person reports in Yosemite Valley alone. At times, serious injury and even death occur. The National Park Service wants everyone's vacation to be as thoroughly rewarding an outdoor experience as possible. Please do not mar your vacation by a lost-child incident. To alleviate such misfortunes, a study of their records reveals that if the following measures are taken, lost-person reports will seldom be necessary.

1. Admonish your children never to leave your sight while wandering about the Park.
2. Tag the small children showing their names, home address, and detailed Park location.
3. Equip each of the children with a whistle before embarking on a hike.
4. Show them, firsthand, the restroom they are to use, and fix in their minds the path they should follow.
5. Have your child repeat your instructions aloud, so you know he understands.

If you need assistance, contact the nearest Park Ranger immediately.

PUBLICATIONS

The Yosemite Natural History Association (P.O. Box 545, Yosemite National Park, California 95389) is a non-profit distributing organization whose purpose is the stimulation of interest in the educational and inspirational aspects of Yosemite's history and natural history. The Association cooperates with and is recognized by the United States Department of the Interior and its Bureau, the National Park Service, as an essential operating organization.

As one means of accomplishing its aims the Association publishes reasonably priced books and booklets which are available for purchase by mail or at the museum's information desks in the Park. The following prices include handling, postage, and the 4 percent California Sales Tax. Orders should be accompanied by check or money order payable to Yosemite Natural History Association. (Postage stamps will not be accepted. Prices subject to change without notice.)

General

Auto Tour of Yosemite National Park–Ditton & McHenry	.90
Backpacking in the Sierra Nevada–Jones	.65
Climber's Guide to High Sierra–Sierra Club	5.15
Devils Postpile National Monument–Hartesveldt	.60
Going Light with Backpack or Burro–Sierra Club	2.80
Illustrated Guide to Yosemite–Adams (paperbound)	3.30
Mammoth Lakes Sierra–Sierra Club	3.25
National Parks in California–Yeager	2.20
Short Line to Paradise, Story of Yosemite Valley Railroad–Johnston (paperbound)	2.20
Starr's Guide to John Muir Trail and High Sierra Region–Sierra Club	2.25
This is Yosemite–Hubbard	1.25
Tuolumne Meadows, Trail Guide to–Shields	.80
Waterfalls of Yosemite and of the World–Brockman	.60
Yosemite Valley–Adams	3.90

Animal Life

Birds of Yosemite–Stebbins	1.20
Fishes of Yosemite National Park–Evans-Wallis	.60

202

Animal Life (*continued*)

Mammals of Yosemite National Park–Parker   .65
Reptiles and Amphibians of Yosemite National Park–
  Walker   .65
Sierra Nevada Natural History   4.30
Yosemite Butterflies–Garth & Tilden (paperbound)   2.20

Trees and Flowers

Broad-leaved Trees of Yosemite National Park–Brockman   .60
Cone-bearing Trees of Yosemite National Park–Cole   .65
Ferns of the Sierra–Rodin   1.15
Giant Sequoias–Cook (paperbound)   .25
Trees of Yosemite National Park–Tresidder & Hoss
  (paperbound)   2.80
Trees of Yosemite National Park–Tresidder & Hoss
  (clothbound)   4.90
Wildflowers of the Sierra–Hubbard   .45

History and Indians

Big Oak Flat Road to Yosemite–Paden & Schlictmann
  (paperbound)   5.20
Big Oak Flat Road to Yosemite–Paden & Schlictmann
  (clothbound)   7.50
Ghost Mines of Yosemite–Hubbard (paperbound)   1.25
Guardians of the Yosemite (Ranger History)–Bingaman   1.75
John Muir, Protector of the Wilds–Haines & Morrill   2.55
Miwok Material Culture–Barrett & Gifford (paperbound)   2.80
Miwok Material Culture–Barrett & Gifford (clothbound)   4.90
100 Years in Yosemite–Russell (paperbound)   2.80
100 Years in Yosemite–Russell (clothbound)   4.90
Tioga Road–1883-1861–Trexler   .60
Wawona's Yesterdays–Sargent   .90
Wilderness World of John Muir–Teale   6.50
Yosemite Indians–Godfrey   .60
Yosemite–Saga of a Century (paperbound)   .90
Yosemite Story–Scott   1.25
Yosemite—Story of an Idea–Huth (paperbound)   .60
Yosemite Yarns (Stagedriver Stories)–Degnan & Hubbard   1.75

(*Continued*)

Geology and Maps

Geology of Yosemite Valley, Brief Story of–Beatty .35
Incomparable Valley–Matthes (paperbound) 2.20
Map of Yosemite National Park, Topographic–USGS .90
Map of Yosemite Valley, Topo.–Geology story printed
on reverse side .65
Quadrangle Maps of Devils Postpile, El Portal, Hetch
Hetchy, Lake Eleanor, Matterhorn, Merced Peak,
Mono Craters, Pinecrest, Tower Peak, Tuolumne
Meadows, and Yosemite @ .65 each .65
South Boundary Country, Pocket Guide to–Clark .45
South Boundary Country, Trail Guide to–Clark .65

For Children

A Day With Tupi, an Indian Boy of the Sierra–Hubbard
(paperbound) 1.25
Animal Friends of the Sierra–Hubbard (paperbound) 1.25

INDEX

213